Far from Heaven

American Indies

Series Editors: Gary Needham and Yannis Tzioumakis

Titles in the series include:

The Spanish Prisoner
Yannis Tzioumakis
978 0 7486 3368 5 (hbk)
978 0 7486 3369 2 (pbk)

Brokeback Mountain
Gary Needham
978 0 7486 3382 1 (hbk)
978 0 7486 3383 8 (pbk)

Memento
Claire Molloy
978 0 7486 3771 3 (hbk)
978 0 7486 3772 0 (pbk)

Lost in Translation
Geoff King
978 0 7486 3745 4 (hbk)
978 0 7486 3746 1 (pbk)

Far from Heaven
Glyn Davis
978 0 7486 3778 2 (hbk)
978 0 7486 3779 9 (pbk)

Forthcoming titles include:

Being John Malkovich
Christine Holmlund
978 0 7486 4193 2 (hbk)
978 0 7486 4192 5 (pbk)

Visit the American Indies website at www.euppublishing.com/series/
amin

Far from Heaven

Glyn Davis

Edinburgh University Press

© Glyn Davis, 2011

Edinburgh University Press Ltd
22 George Square, Edinburgh

www.euppublishing.com

Typeset in 11/13pt Monotype Baskerville by
Servis Filmsetting Ltd, Stockport, Cheshire, and
printed and bound in Great Britain by
CPI Antony Rowe, Chippenham and Eastbourne

A CIP record for this book is available from the British Library

ISBN 978 0 7486 3778 2 (hardback)
ISBN 978 0 7486 3779 9 (paperback)

The right of Glyn Davis
to be identified as author of this work
has been asserted in accordance with
the Copyright, Designs and Patents Act 1988.

Grateful acknowledgement is made for permission to reproduce material previously published elsewhere. Every effort has been made to trace the copyright holders, but if any have been inadvertently overlooked, the publisher will be pleased to make the necessary arrangements at the first opportunity.

Contents

Series Preface

In recent years American independent cinema has not only become the focus of significant scholarly attention but as a category of film it has shifted from a marginal to a central position within American cinema – a shift that can be also detected in the emergence of the label 'indie' cinema as opposed to independent cinema. The popularisation of this 'indie' brand of filmmaking began in the 1990s with the commercial success of the Sundance Film Festival and of specialty distributor Miramax Films, as well as the introduction of DVD, which made independent films more readily available as well as profitable for the first time. At the same time, film studies started developing courses that distinguished American independent cinema from mainstream Hollywood, treating it as a separate object of study and a distinct discursive category.

Despite the surge in interest in independent cinema, a surge that involved the publication of at least twenty books and edited collections alongside a much larger number of articles on various aspects of independent cinema, especially about the post-1980 era, the field – as it has developed – still remains greatly under-researched in relation to the changes of the past twenty years that define the shift from independent to 'indie' cinema. This is partly because a multifaceted phenomenon such as American independent cinema, the history of which is as long and complex as the history of mainstream Hollywood, has yet to be adequately and satisfactorily documented. In this respect, academic film criticism is still in great need to account for the plethora of shapes, forms and guises that American independent cinema has manifested itself in. This is certainly not an easy task given that independent film has, indeed, taken a wide variety of forms at different historical trajectories and has been influenced by a hugely diverse range of factors.

It is with this problem in mind that 'American Indies' was conceived by its editors. While the history of American independent cinema is still being written with more studies already set to be published in the forthcoming years, and while journal articles are enhancing our understanding of more focused aspects of independent filmmaking, the 'American Indies' series has been created to provide the necessary space to explore and engage with specific examples of American 'indie' films in a great depth. Through this format, 'American Indies' aims to encourage an examination of both the 'indie' text and its contexts, of understanding how 'indie' films operate within a particular filmmaking practice but also how 'indies' have been shaping a new formation of American cinema. In this respect, 'American Indies' provides the space for a detailed examination of industrial, economic and institutional concerns alongside the more usual formal and aesthetic considerations that have historically characterised critical approaches of independent films. 'American Indies' is a series of comprehensive studies of carefully selected examples of recent films that reveal in great detail the many sides of the phenomenon of the recently emerged American 'indie' cinema.

As the first book series to explore and define this aspect of American cinema, 'American Indies' has had the extremely difficult task of producing a comprehensive set of criteria that informs its selection of titles. Given the vastness of the field, we have made several editorial decisions in order to produce a coherent definition of this new phase of American independent cinema. The first such choice was to concentrate on recent examples of independent cinema. Although the word 'recent' has often been used to include films made in the post-1980 period, as editors we decided that the cut off point for films to be included in this series would be the year 1996. This was an extremely significant year in the independent film sector, 'the year of the independents' as was triumphantly proclaimed by the *Los Angeles Business Journal* in February 1997, for a number of reasons. Arguably, the most significant of these reasons was the dynamic entrance in the film market of Fox Searchlight, a new type of a specialty film division created by 20th Century Fox in 1995 with the explicit intention of claiming a piece of the increasingly large independent film market pie. Fox Searchlight would achieve this objective through the production and distribution of films that followed many of the conventions of independent film as those were established after the success of *sex, lies and videotape* in 1989. These conventions had since then started being popularised by a number of films produced and distributed by Miramax Films, an independent company that was taken over by Disney after the phenomenal box-office success of several of its films at approximately the same time as 20th Century Fox was establishing its specialty division.

The now direct involvement of entertainment conglomerates like Disney and Fox in the independent film sector had far-reaching effects. Arguably, the most important of these was that the label 'independent', which for critics and the cinema going public (wrongly) signified economic independence from major film companies like Disney, Fox, Paramount, Universal, etc., obviously ceased to convey this meaning. Instead, critics and public alike started using increasingly the label 'indie' which suggested a particular type of film that adhered to a set of conventions as well as a transformed independent cinema sector that was now driven by specialty companies, most of which subsidiaries of major entertainment conglomerates. It is this form of 'independent' cinema that has produced some of the most interesting films to come out from American cinema in recent years that 'American Indies' has set out to explore in great depth and which explains our selection of the label 'indies' instead of independents.

We hope readers will enjoy the series

Gary Needham and Yannis Tzioumakis
American Indies Series Editors

Acknowledgements

First and foremost, my thanks to series editors Gary Needham and Yannis Tzioumakis. It was they who invited me to write on *Far from Heaven* – and who later handled with great patience and sensitivity my repeated requests for extensions to deadlines. They have been exceptional to work with on this project and made the book a pleasure to write.

This book also owes a great deal to a number of people who, during its writing, have provided intellectual and moral sustenance, banter, caffeine, provocative suggestions and useful pointers. Kay Dickinson read chunks of this manuscript at various points; my writing and thinking always owe immeasurable amounts to her. Karen Lury coerced me into confronting and working through some of the difficult conceptual issues that this project presented for me – and this book is all the better for it. At Glasgow School of Art, I would like to thank several of my colleagues who have provided backing and encouragement for my research and writing, as well as some fantastic resources and lateral connections I would never have unearthed on my own: Nicky Bird, Laura Gonzalez, Sarah Smith and Damian Sutton. Finally, two extra-special thanks. I have probably spent more time talking to Gary Needham, my queer theory ally, about Todd Haynes and *Far from Heaven* than anyone else I know. As with all of the other projects we have sustained and backed each other through, his perceptive insights and breadth of knowledge never cease to astound me. Iain Barbour, with his seemingly unending patience, understanding and love, has provided all of the most important kinds of props, encouragement and distractions during the writing of this book, from retreats in the Highlands of Scotland to episodes of *Project Runway*. Without him, this book would be so much less – and so would I.

Introduction

Towards the end of Todd Haynes's *Far from Heaven* (2002), Frank Whitaker (Dennis Quaid) comes home unexpectedly early. Sitting in the living room of the immaculate suburban home he shares with his family, he begins to cry, then makes a confession to his wife Cathy (Julianne Moore): 'I've fallen in love with someone, who wants to be with me.' The 'someone' is a handsome blond man. 'I tried so hard to make it go away,' he stammers to Cathy, referring to his homosexuality. The audience is not surprised – they earlier witnessed Frank's cruising and seduction of the other chap – but Cathy seems shell-shocked, the camera slowly dollying towards her as she stands static, numb, her face immobile. After a pause, she says, softly, 'I assume, then, you'll be wanting a divorce.' Let me begin this book with a confession of my own, which may leave you shell-shocked: the first time I watched *Far from Heaven* I thought it was, well, far from heavenly. This came as a surprise to me, as I am a committed fan of Haynes and a devotee of the career of Julianne Moore, and adore the 1950s Douglas Sirk melodramas to which the film pays sustained homage. But the film left me cold, numb, and so I tried hard to make it go away, divorce myself from it.

Several things initially bothered me about *Far from Heaven*: the seeming loss of Haynes's authorial imprint; what I diagnosed as a rigorous and clinical adherence to the 'classical melodrama' genre template without experiment; and the apparently rather conservative nature of the film's identity politics. Now, several years and countless re-viewings of the film later, I can barely believe my initial response to it (let alone bring myself to confess it out loud). The aspects of the film which concerned me are, I swiftly came to realise – and as this book will explore – its most interesting and provocative. And such is the film's power to move me now that even the DVD menu, with a soft extract from Elmer Bernstein's score playing over an abstracted image of autumnal leaves drifting from trees, can bring tears to my eyes.

This book will argue that *Far from Heaven* is one of the most significant American independent films of the last twenty years, a major milestone in the career of its director, and a provocative and challenging piece of work that is, like all of Haynes's other movies, deeply political. On the surface, of course, the film seems simple and straightforward. In 1950s Hartford, Connecticut, housewife Cathy discovers her husband is gay; although he has medical treatment for his 'condition', it is unsuccessful and he eventually leaves her. Meanwhile, Cathy develops a friendship with, and slowly falls for, her black gardener Raymond (Dennis Haysbert). Town gossip drives a wedge between them, however, and Raymond decides to leave Hartford for Baltimore. The whole film, from set design to score, lighting to costume, is made in the style of one of the melodramas that Douglas Sirk directed for Universal in the 1950s – *Magnificent Obsession* (1954), *All That Heaven Allows* (1955), *Written on the Wind* (1956), *Imitation of Life* (1959) – giving it a seamless, flawless sheen. However, the tension between neat surface appearance and churning hidden emotions is not only one of the main narrative themes of *Far from Heaven*; it also relates more broadly to the relationship between the polished and dazzling film and the deeper ideas and concerns with which it engages.

Far from Heaven is Todd Haynes's most successful film to date in terms of reviews from critics, box office receipts, level of distribution, and awards. The website metacritic.com, which compiles and aggregates reviews, records an average score of 84 out of 100 for *Far from Heaven*. Many reviewers gushed about the film. Owen Gleiberman in *Entertainment Weekly*, for instance, said it was 'bold and brilliant'; David Sterritt, in *Christian Science Monitor*, called it 'easily the best American film so far this year' and judged it to be 'close to perfect.'[1] At the global box office, it took more than twice its budget in ticket sales. At the peak of its release in the United States, *Far from Heaven* was showing in 291 theatres. This may seem low compared with major studio films, which often screen in thousands of auditoria when in wide release across North America, but is worth comparing with Haynes's previous two films, *Velvet Goldmine* (eighty-five US screens) and *Safe* (sixteen US screens). The film premiered at the Venice Film Festival in 2002, at which Julianne Moore won the Audience Award for Best Actress and the Volpi Cup for Best Actress. *Far from Heaven* was subsequently nominated for four

Academy Awards – for best actress (Moore), best original screenplay (Haynes), best cinematography (Edward Lachman) and best music (Bernstein) – and nominated for four Golden Globe awards – best actress, best supporting actor (Quaid), best screenplay and best original score.

As these plaudits suggest, *Far from Heaven* was the film which provided Todd Haynes with a wider level of public and critical recognition than he had ever previously attained. As Richard Falcon noted in *Sight and Sound*, 'Its success in the United States has shifted Haynes' career up a gear, from indie festival favourite to mainstream acclaim.'[2] In this introduction, I will provide a brief overview of that career, and some factual detail regarding the genesis of *Far from Heaven*. I will also outline the structure of this book, and the major topics and theoretical concerns that each chapter explores.

Todd Haynes first garnered a certain level of public visibility as a filmmaker through controversy. Following the production of his graduation film *Assassins* (1985), which centred on the life and writings of the French poet Arthur Rimbaud, he worked on a forty-three-minute biopic, *Superstar: The Karen Carpenter Story* (1987), which told the story of the singer's career using Barbie-like dolls and hand-made sets. Although this film circulated above ground for several years, with screenings taking place in art galleries, cinemas and other spaces, it was pulled from legitimate distribution in 1990 when the Carpenter estate objected to its unapproved use of songs by the group, and sent Haynes legal cease-and-desist letters. *Superstar* still exchanges hands in heavily bootlegged VHS and DVD form, and is occasionally shown (illicitly) in cinemas. The controversy continued with Haynes's first full-length feature, *Poison* (1991), which wove together three separate narrative strands, all inspired by the writings of Jean Genet: a pastiche black-and-white horror story, a men-in-prison drama, and a documentary about a young boy who shoots his father and then, it seems, flies away. Made for around $250,000, a significant percentage of which came from grants, *Poison* was the grand prize-winner at the 1991 Sundance Film Festival. The film's release, however, led to a right-wing conservative backlash, with a number of commentators (some of whom had clearly not seen the film) decrying the use of public funds to support the production of 'gay pornography'.[3]

Poison appeared around the same time – and at similar festivals – as a number of other low-budget, formally experimental films which unapologetically focused on non-heterosexual 'deviants' and their transgressive behaviours. These titles included Tom Kalin's debut feature *Swoon* (1992), Gregg Araki's *The Living End* (1992), Derek Jarman's *Edward II* (1991), Sadie Benning's pixelvision shorts, and a host of others. In an article first published in 1992, these films were dubbed 'New Queer Cinema' by film critic B. Ruby Rich, a label that stuck (and which a number of the directors associated with the movement subsequently tried to shake off).[4] This movement or moment, although it had international roots, became one of the most important and notable strands of American 'indie' film throughout the 1990s, leading eventually to mainstream Hollywood dalliances with unsympathetic queer protagonists (in films such as *The Talented Mr Ripley* [Minghella, 1999]) and to breakthrough 'indie' titles including *Boys Don't Cry* (Peirce, 1999).

Haynes followed up *Poison* with a short film for television, *Dottie Gets Spanked* (1993), before making *Safe* in 1995, the narrative of which centres on Carol White (Julianne Moore), a suburb-dwelling 'home-maker' who develops 'environmental illness' and ends up moving to an isolated commune. Haynes's subsequent film was *Velvet Goldmine* (1998), a movie about glam rock that is part coming-of-age story, part music biopic, part journalist-uncovering-a-story drama and part grey dystopian science fiction, but also includes colourful fantasy sequences such as the delivery of baby Oscar Wilde to his parents by a UFO. The film fared poorly at the box office, and received mixed reviews. As Christine Vachon, head of Killer Films and Haynes's associate since early in his filmmaking career, has written:

In 1999 Todd Haynes went into a creative funk after *Velvet Goldmine*. He'd spent six months living in London making a beautiful, difficult, risky film about glam rock only to come back and find out nobody cared about it nearly as much as we did. Not Miramax, who halfheartedly distributed it, not the critics, who called it 'overambitious' and 'maddening', and not audiences. We spent $9 million – then the biggest budget in Killer's history – on huge sets in Brixton, Ewan McGregor's paycheck, and about five hundred pairs of platform shoes. *Velvet Goldmine* made $1.5 million. That's not great math.[5]

Haynes was clearly hit hard by the poor distribution and reception of the film, especially after the lengthy and fraught process of making it. Drastic moves were needed in order to improve his mood. As Ella Taylor reports in an interview with Haynes,

Disillusioned by life in New York, which he felt had grown too cleaned-up and professional, and with his mood unelevated by reading 'all of Proust' during his year off, the director got into his car in early 2000 and drove almost without stopping to Portland, Oregon, where his sister had found him a lovely Victorian house to occupy for a few months. 'It was this strangely dry winter and spring in Portland – it just rained flower petals for four months. It was very Sirkian, very lush.'[6]

Haynes was revitalised in Portland – also the home of New Queer Cinema director Gus Van Sant, with whom he spent time socially. As Robert Sullivan writes, 'For Todd Haynes, Portland was a tonic. It's a lo-fi town, a do-it-yourselfer's paradise, a place where, in contrast to New York, your career is not necessarily everything. "When I moved to Portland, I was more social and productive than I'd ever been in my entire life," Haynes says.'[7] In the autumn of 2000, Haynes called Vachon and told her about his idea for a new project: he wanted to write a Sirkian melodrama. The screenplay was written very swiftly, in somewhere between ten days and four weeks (reports differ). 'In a weird way,' says Haynes, 'it was a commencement piece to my sadness, so it resulted more from something I was looking back at than from the new feeling of birth and revitalisation I felt in Portland. But the script poured out of me. Which of course made me completely mistrust it. I thought, "This must be crap." '[8] Vachon has also commented on the writing of the *Far from Heaven* script:

Usually Todd labours a lot more over things. The script for *Velvet Goldmine*, for example, started out at about 250 pages and went through nine months of rewrites. But this script flowed out. He sends it to me with a beautiful cover drawing he did himself in coloured pencil of Cathy, the main character, with a scarf over her head. [. . .] The script is so simple and flawless, I say 'There's not much you can do to this.'[9]

Vachon states that the one recommendation she made was to remove a blowjob – Cathy was going to discover her husband's sexual proclivities by walking in on Frank performing fellatio:

On one level, I love it because it is this moment that rips everything open [. . .] Rock Hudson often starred in Sirk's films . . . and the idea that you'd see Rock Hudson going down on Robert Stack in a Sirk movie is *wild*. But it would have blown Cathy's mind and perhaps our rating. So Todd downgrades the contact to a deep kiss. Other than that, what you would eventually see on screen is the draft published to me.[10]

A number of other alterations and minor changes were made during the early stages. Haynes toyed with calling the film *This Splendid Life*, *Circles in the Sun*, *Fall from Splendour* and *The Surface of Things*, before deciding on *Far from Heaven*. The first version of the script had Cathy talking to Frank about an uncle she had who was 'different'. But Haynes gave the script to Richard Glatzer to read. (Glatzer directed *Grief* (1993), and co-directed *The Fluffer* (2001) and *Echo Park, L.A.* (2006) with Wash Westmoreland, the latter of which Haynes executive-produced.) Glatzer suggested cutting Cathy's confession, saying that she wouldn't be able to talk about it and would remain evasive.[11] The published screenplay of *Far from Heaven* also includes a number of elements which did not make it to the final cut – most notably, an end voiceover delivered by Cathy as she leaves the train station.[12]

. . .

This book is divided into four main chapters, each of which outlines different ways of thinking through and about *Far from Heaven*. Chapter 1 begins with an historical overview of the shifting landscape of independent cinema in the United States over the last twenty years, charting, in particular, the development of the realm known as 'Indiewood'. The remainder of the chapter then explores *Far from Heaven*'s status as an 'independent' movie, identifying key characteristics of the film that enable or trouble its categorisation as such: the size of the budget, the style of the film, the actors cast in the main roles, and so on. The discussion also, through considering these characteristics, provides an account of the production history of the film, from the pre-production stage through to its release into cinemas.

Chapter 2 engages with the notion of authorship – a central concern for Film Studies scholars since the inauguration of debates about auteurism in the 1950s. *Far from Heaven* was marketed and advertised to audiences as 'a Todd Haynes film', and part of the chapter is thus devoted to identifying the ways in which the movie repeats or echoes thematic concerns and stylistic devices used by Haynes in his earlier films. And yet, *Far from Heaven* also challenges such traditional models of authorship. As the film is a meticulous simulation of a style and narrative form associated with another director, Douglas Sirk, does this 'de-authorise' Haynes's input? Further, given that *Far from Heaven* is also a heavily intertextual pastiche – as are many other 'indie' movies of the last twenty years, such as *Reservoir Dogs* (Tarantino, 1992) – how does this affect understandings of the film as the unique vision of its director?

In Chapter 3, the focus turns to genre. Compared with other films by Todd Haynes, *Far from Heaven* is notable for not mixing and matching genres. An outline of the main aspects of the 'family melodrama' is provided, along with an exploration of how neatly Haynes's film fits the generic template. In fact, *Far from Heaven* was only one of a number of films made in the first years of the twenty-first century that revisited the genre of the melodrama. But why were these films made at this particular time? Arguments are made to suggest that *Far from Heaven* invited audiences to contemplate how swiftly genres mutate or become outmoded, and to reflect on how the experience of crying at the cinema is now a rare occurrence. Indeed, sustained attention is paid to the significance of crying in relation to *Far from Heaven* – the mechanisms used by the film to induce tears from viewers, and the spectacle of crying on display in the movie. Finally, picking up on threads running through the chapter, attention is concentrated on the relationship between gay men and mainstream melodrama. The lack of representation of gay characters in melodrama is contrasted with the devotion of many gay spectators to the genre, with explanations offered for both phenomena.

Finally, Chapter 4 examines in detail the queerness of *Far from Heaven*. Following an introduction to the term 'queer', and a brief overview of the history of queer politics and queer theory, four main topics are explored. Firstly, a history of queer underground/experimental/art-house/independent film appropriations of the melodrama is provided, followed by identification of how Haynes's film can be seen as part of this lineage. Secondly, the role of particular supporting characters (Eleanor, Mona, Sybil) in contributing to the film's queerness is outlined. Thirdly, drawing on Alexander Doty's arguments about queer reading practices and Patricia White's notion of 'retrospectatorship', *Far from Heaven*'s impact on audience understandings and interpretations of examples of classical melodrama is explored. Finally, a reading of *Far from Heaven* as an AIDS movie is proposed.

1. 'Indie'

One of the main aims of the 'American Indies' book series, to which this monograph belongs, is to explore the shifting parameters of 'independent' US cinema over the course of the last twenty years. This subject underpins this book, as the discussions in individual chapters are all dedicated to concerns often associated with 'independence' in film practice and production: directorial authorship, adherence to/ divergence from generic form, political messages and intentions. However, this first chapter will concentrate specifically on the field of American independent cinema, and *Far from Heaven*'s position within that context. The chapter begins with a short historical overview which charts the movement from independent American cinema of the 1980s, to the development of 'Indiewood' as a hybrid field of production. Subsequent sections then consider specific aspects of *Far from Heaven* that could be seen as marking Haynes's film as 'independent': the budget, casting and acting style; its distinctive aesthetic; and its attention to issues of identity politics. In these later parts of the chapter, information about the film's gestation, production, distribution and exhibition will be introduced. In other words, this chapter has two main aims: to consider what makes an American film 'independent' in the first years of the twenty-first century, and to provide an outline of *Far from Heaven*'s making.

From Independent to Indiewood

Independent cinema is not a recent phenomenon in the American film landscape. As Chuck Kleinhans writes, 'Independent production and diffusion . . . was the norm when cinema was starting. But by the 1920s a dominant structure, the Hollywood studio system, was firmly in place, and all other cinematic expressions existed in some kind of relationship to it.'[1] For much of the twentieth century, independent cinema in the United States provided an alternative to the practices and output of the major studios, from the films made by the Poverty Row outfits from the 1930s to the 1950s, to those produced by exploitation companies such as American International Pictures and William Castle Productions in the 1950s and 1960s.[2] As Kleinhans puts it, ' "Independent" . . . has to be understood as a relational term – independent in relation to the dominant system – rather than taken as indicating a practice that is totally free-standing and autonomous.'[3] Further, the forms that American independent cinema has taken have varied widely; as Geoff King has noted, they include (but are not limited to) avant-garde and experimental works, those with political or polemical content, exploitation cinema and 'stylish, cultish, or offbeat films'.[4] However, the division between the fields of independent and mainstream production has never been stable or clearly maintained. Independent companies have become major players (as occurred, for instance, with Disney); some filmmakers have moved between working on low-budget independent fare and major studio pictures; 'independent' films can be as generic as Hollywood movies, and often adhere to the classical narrative template normally associated with the output of the major studios.

Since the 1980s, this blurring has become more pronounced. This is largely due to significant changes in the organisation of the American film industry: independent production and distribution companies gaining power and status; major studios buying up successful independent organisations, or establishing their own specialty divisions with an objective to trade and operate in the independent film market. These developments deserve brief attention, in order to establish the context within which *Far from Heaven* was made and distributed; they have all contributed to the formation of a landscape in which attempting to identify a film as 'independent' on the basis of its budget, content or aesthetics is necessarily fraught and complex – if not impossible.

The 1980s – the decade in which Todd Haynes began his filmmaking career – are often identified by critics and theorists as a boom period for independent filmmaking in the United States. An infrastructure which supported the production and distribution of independent work solidified throughout the decade. Robert Redford's Sundance Institute was formed in 1981 to support independent filmmakers. The US Film Festival, started in 1978 to support 'small regional films', was taken over by Sundance in 1984, and grew in stature and profile in subsequent years.[5] The Independent Feature Project (IFP) was launched in 1979 as a forum to support independent filmmakers; its annual market became an important focus for directors and producers to raise awareness of (and funds for) their work. A significant number of independent distribution companies launched, including the Samuel Goldwyn Company (in 1978) and Castle Hill Productions (in 1980).[6] A boom in cable television and home video throughout the 1980s led to increased opportunities for independent cinema. As Geoff King notes,

Penetration of video recorders into US households increased from three per cent in 1980 to nearly 75 per cent in 1989, creating an enormous demand for product. Total revenue from pre-recorded cassette rentals and sales grew from $76 million to an estimated $7 billion in the same period. Video companies seeking product to keep up with the demand became a major component of independent film financing.[7]

In addition, as David Rosen identifies, there was a greater availability of investment capital in the Reaganite economy of the 1980s, from which independent filmmakers (with their typically low budgets) could benefit.[8] All of these developments contributed to a surge in independent film production; as Justin Wyatt specifies, 'independent films increased from 193 in 1986 to 277 in 1987 and to 393 in 1988.'[9]

John Pierson identifies 1989 as the year when the major studios started to take a serious interest in cinema made independently.[10] Following the commercial and critical success of *sex, lies and videotape* (Soderbergh, 1989), in particular, the main Hollywood corporations began to recognise independent cinema as a valuable source of income, of talent, of titles that they could distribute, and of companies with whom they could forge alliances. Some independent film organisations became large and powerful on the back of particular successes, in combination with sophisticated business expansion tactics. Miramax, for instance, founded in 1979, distributed *sex, lies and videotape*, and attained widespread recognition with a slate of releases that included *The Grifters* (Frears, 1990), *In Bed with Madonna* (Keshishian, 1991), *Reservoir Dogs* (Tarantino, 1991) and *The Crying Game* (Jordan, 1992). Miramax became associated with controversy in the late 1980s and early 1990s; as Justin Wyatt identifies, they 'repeatedly . . . maximised the publicity created by challenging the MPAA ratings system', fighting battles over the ratings of films such as *Tie Me Up! Tie Me Down!* (Almodóvar, 1990).[11] The company also successfully employed advertising tactics that emphasised the broader appeal of niche or art-house titles; *The Crying Game*, for instance, was sold as a thriller, downplaying its political components, while the trailer for *Pulp Fiction* (Tarantino, 1994) created 'an image . . . of the film as being full of action, comedy and sex'.[12] As a second example, New Line Cinema was founded in 1967 as a distribution company, but moved into production in the 1970s and 1980s. It had notable successes with the *Nightmare on Elm Street* franchise and with the distribution of *Teenage Mutant Ninja Turtles* (Barron, 1990). Both of these companies threatened to dominate the independent production and distribution sector as they wielded increasing financial power; they also demonstrated the substantial audience interest in independent films, and the money that could be made in the sector. Miramax was bought by Disney in 1993, and New Line by Ted Turner's Turner Broadcasting System in the same year.

In addition to the major studios buying up or merging with independent production and distribution companies, they have also formed their own divisions for supporting films with lower budgets than the standard 'blockbuster' releases. These specialty arms, or 'classics divisions', experienced a first flourish in the 1980s, with companies such as 20th Century Fox International Classics (1982–4) distributing art films from countries outside of the United States and low-budget American independent features. A second much more substantial wave began in the mid-1990s, when, as Yannis Tzioumakis notes, 'the majors moved into the establishment of a new breed of classics divisions, which financed as well as distributed relatively low-budget films. These new classics tried clearly to emulate the phenomenal success of Miramax.'[13] These specialty arms included Sony Pictures Classics (in operation from 1992 to date), Fox Searchlight (1994 to date) and Focus Features (2002 to date). The different classics divisions have attempted to construct distinct identities in relation to each other, and they have differing levels of freedom and independence from their parent studios.

It is worth dwelling briefly on Focus Features, as the first title card that appears before *Far from Heaven* is for Focus; they were responsible for distributing Haynes's film in the United States. The history of Focus Features, the specialty wing of Universal, is tangled and complex, but demonstrates the concerted efforts made by the major studios in order to secure a slice of the 'independent' sector. As Geoff King summarises, Universal bought the notable specialty distributor October Films in 1997 and was also involved in Gramercy Pictures, as a joint venture with Polygram Filmed Entertainment. Gramercy subsequently became part of USA Films, a division of USA Networks, as did October; they all came back together under the same umbrella in December 2000, when USA Networks was merged with Universal's then corporate parent, Vivendi. In the meantime, the 'Focus' identity came into its first incarnation as the specialty unit, Universal Focus. In 2002 Universal bought another noted independent outfit, Good Machine, and folded it and USA Films into the new-look Focus Features.[14]

Although Focus Features, according to King, 'has less autonomy from its studio parent than rivals such as Miramax . . . and Sony Pictures Classics',[15] it is significant that its first heads were David Linde and James Schamus, who came from USA Films and Good Machine respectively. As Gary Needham notes, 'both these companies had an established pedigree and expertise, which was immediately brought in to Focus: Good Machine's track record in foreign sales operations complemented well USA Films' healthy production slate.'[16] Good Machine, in addition, was a key production and distribution outfit in the independent American cinema scene of the 1990s, involved in the production of (amongst others) Todd Haynes's *Safe* (1995) and Todd Solondz's *Happiness* (1998). Needham identifies that Linde and Schamus swiftly established Focus Features as 'a quality brand with prestige and kudos', and with 'a strong investment in authorship and left-field productions'.[17]

With 'independent' films now being financed and distributed by studio subsidiaries such as Focus Features, by 'mini-majors' like Lionsgate, and outside the purview and influence of such organisations, the term itself has arguably lost some of its meaning. As Tzioumakis writes,

the use of the label 'independent' has become increasingly difficult to sustain, and new, more ambiguous labels such as 'indie' (short for independent, but also signifying a film that could have been produced and/or distributed by any major independent or classics division) and 'indiewood' ('a grey area' between Hollywood and the independent sector) have become staples of the vocabulary used by filmmakers, film critics and industry analysts alike.[18]

Christine Holmlund makes a similar observation:

With so many expensive independent feature films now produced and released by mini-majors and the majors' own independent arms, independent films would seem to have moved squarely to the mainstream, away from the margins where historically they served to supplement studio production and often expressed 'outsider' perspectives. Has 'indie' become merely a brand, a label used to market biggish budget productions that aim to please many by offending few?[19]

Certainly, it could be argued that 'indie' has become simply a genre of cinema, financed both within and outside of the studio system; films such as Fox Searchlight's *Juno* (Reitman, 2007) and *(500) Days of Summer* (Webb, 2009), for instance, adopt or appropriate aesthetic strategies (idiosyncratic soundtrack, fractured narrative form, excessive formal flourishes, and so on) that were previously used almost exclusively by filmmakers operating outside of the Hollywood studio system.

This is not to say, of course, that independent cinema made entirely outside of the major studios does not still appear or gain attention. And the notion of independent cinema as a source of material that offers an alternative – formal, aesthetic, ideological – to the mainstream arguably persists as an important ideal. However, with the emergence of a number of well-capitalised producers and distributors without formal ties to the studios, and the encroachment of the major studios on to the 'independent' scene, attaining funding and distribution for a truly independent film has become increasingly difficult. As Chris Holmlund wrote in 2005,

for those who are most on the margins, without production backing or distribution help from majors or mini-majors – i.e. the majority of documentarians, everyone who makes avant-garde work, and the many young and old hopefuls (in particular African Americans, Latinos, Asian Americans, and/or women) who helm short and feature fiction films – the situation today is far worse than when the current indie boom began in the late 1970s and early 1980s. State and federals funding have dried up, and although there are now literally hundreds of festivals screening independent films, only a few – Sundance and Toronto prime among them – net pickups. [. . .] Compounding the problem is the fact that the more important festivals now serve as 'glitzy launching pads' for films specialty distributors have themselves produced.[20]

A useful example here would be Diane Bell's film *Obselidia* (2010). Despite a number of years working within the Hollywood studio system, Bell was unable to attain interest in, or funding to produce, her movie script. With the assistance of creative personnel she had met at the studios – cameramen, cinematographers, and so on – who were willing to work for very little, she financed the film herself for around $200,000. The film went on to win two awards at the 2010 Sundance Festival: the Alfred P. Sloan Feature Film prize and a gong for Excellence in Cinematography. To date, however, *Obselidia* has not been picked up for distribution, either to cinemas or direct to DVD; like many independent films made outside of the studio system, it has failed to circulate beyond the festival circuit.[21]

At first viewing *Far from Heaven* does not necessarily seem like an independent film. It features stars of a particular calibre; it has a lush orchestral score by Elmer Bernstein; the narrative structure is linear and modelled on a classical Hollywood template; the cinematography, set design, costume and décor are meticulous and sumptuous; it is distributed by Focus Features. However, there are also markers of independence: the size of the budget, as the film clearly did not cost an extraordinary amount; the casting, which includes some provocative choices; the acting style, which is removed from contemporary standards of realism; the distinctive look of the film; and the attention to identity politics (female, gay, black). These five issues, which will be used to structure the remainder of this chapter, deserve particular consideration, as they highlight the ways in which the distinctions between independent film production outside of the studio system, 'indie' cinema as a genre or brand, and lower-budget films financed and supported by the classics divisions of the mainstream studios have somewhat dissolved in recent decades.

Budget and Financing

Arguably, one key marker of a film's status as 'independent' is the size of its budget. Throughout the history of film practice in the United States, independent work has regularly been made on budgets a fraction of the size of those available to directors and producers working for the studios. In recent years, however, as the definition of what constitutes 'independent cinema' has become blurred, this distinction has become somewhat hazy. As Tzioumakis identifies,

Independent production companies like IEG are in a position to finance films budgeted in excess of $100 million away from the majors. Independent distributors like the Independent Film Channel Films (IFC Films) score $241.4 million in the US box office with a $5 million production like *My Big Fat Greek Wedding*

(J. Zwick, 2002) . . . Major independents like New Line Cinema produce and distribute *The Lord of the Rings*, a franchise that has brought approximately $1 billion net profit.[22]

In addition, the range of titles financed and distributed by the classics divisions – which now account for a significant percentage of those films reaching audiences which are branded or marketed as 'indie' – have raised the size of the average budget of this sector of production. Despite these developments, independent cinema (whether made within the studios, on their periphery or outside of them) normally has a budget lower than wider-appeal mainstream studio fare.

A major studio release will now cost anywhere between $100 million and $200 million to produce. *Iron Man* (Favreau, 2008) had a budget of $140 million, *2012* (Emmerich, 2009) $200 million and *Inception* (Nolan, 2010) $160 million. In contrast, the films financed by the specialty arms of the studios, such as Focus Features and Paramount Vantage, will be made for a fraction of this cost, usually somewhere in the $10 million to $20 million bracket. *Brokeback Mountain* (Lee, 2005) had a budget of $14 million, *Milk* (Van Sant, 2008) was made for $20 million, and *The Crazies* (Eisner, 2010) also cost $20 million.[23] However, many non-studio independent films are made for much less, with their finances patched together from an array of disparate sources. As Chuck Kleinhans writes,

financing production for independents is significantly different than for major studio projects. The majors finance a project up front and monitor progress to make sure that budgets are being met. In contrast, independents almost always finance production from a variety of sources in a series of stages before distribution is secured. Money is cobbled together.[24]

Guerrilla productions may be entirely personally financed by the film-maker using a variety of means, enabling full control over the film's content and form; for others, some externally sourced funding may provide the impetus to begin filming, with additional monies being sourced where possible.

The directors of independent films often concede how little their films were made for and how they managed to keep costs low. Kevin Smith's film *Clerks* (1994) was made for around $27,000. In order to raise the funds, Smith sold his comic book collection, used a number of credit cards to their full limit, drew on monies set aside for his college education, and deferred salary payments for all of those involved in making the film. *Clerks* is set almost entirely in and around the convenience store in which Smith worked, which he used as a free location; he could only shoot there when the store was closed, and so built this factor into the narrative of the film. In order to keep costs down, Smith cast family members and childhood friends in many of the roles, used only one 16 mm camera, shot in black and white, and completed the shoot in twenty-one days.[25] In contrast, David Lynch's *Eraserhead* (1976) took years to make. Production began with the writing of a short script in 1971 and finance was provided by an American Film Institute grant of $10,000, with extra cash coming from friends and family, including the actress Sissy Spacek. However, Lynch quickly ran out of money and had to work odd jobs to raise any additional finances; the final budget for the film was in the region of $20,000. The making of *Eraserhead* became a weekend-only venture, with individual shots that make up complete scenes in the finished film actually shot years apart from each other.[26] For some independent movies, these budgets might seem enormous. Jonathan Caouette's *Tarnation* (2003) was originally made for under $220, using free iMovie software on a Mac computer to edit together still photographs, Super 8 material, VHS tape, and sound files. (Admittedly, the $220 sum is a false one: in order to bring the film to audiences, the distributor who picked up *Tarnation* had to spend around $400,000 on such aspects as music rights clearances and print production.)[27]

Far from Heaven was initially conceived outside of the studio system. The film's main producer was Christine Vachon, with whom Haynes had previously worked on *Poison* (1991), *Safe* and *Velvet Goldmine* (1998). Vachon is a well-known figure in American independent film production. She is the founder and president of Killer Films, and first made a name for herself by producing a number of titles associated with New Queer Cinema, including *Poison, Swoon* (Kalin, 1992), *Go Fish* (Troche, 1994) and *Postcards from America* (McLean, 1994). She has always remained committed to supporting film projects that tackle issues of queer identity and politics, and the roster of such films that Killer has made include *Stonewall* (Finch, 1995), *I Shot Andy Warhol* (Harron, 1996), *Boys Don't Cry* (Peirce, 1999), *Hedwig and the Angry Inch* (Mitchell, 2001), *Party Monster* (Bailey and Barbato, 2003) and *A Dirty Shame* (Waters, 2004). However, over the last twenty years, Vachon has also produced films by other key figures in independent cinema, including Robert

Altman (*The Company*, 2003), Todd Solondz (*Happiness*, 1998; *Storytelling*, 2001) and Larry Clark (*Kids*, 1995).

The initial budget for *Far from Heaven* was $12 million – the largest budget that Haynes had worked with to date. Vachon had twelve months in which to arrange and secure these finances. John Sloss, the lawyer for Killer Films, recommended spreading the risk and approaching a triumvirate of companies. The first $4 million was secured from Clear Blue Sky, the film financing company owned by Microsoft founder Paul Allen and run by his sister Jody Patton. Although Clear Blue Sky had invested in some films which lost them money – such as Julie Taymor's Shakespeare adaptation *Titus* (1999) – they signed up on the basis of Haynes's script. At Cannes in 2001, Vachon also courted ARP, a French distribution company, who were very enthusiastic about the project. Over the following months, however, ARP failed to confirm their financial investment. As the date of production drew close, Vachon approached TF1, the French television channel, from whom she secured international support and finance.

Vachon wanted to attract the final third of the financing from a North American distributor, and so sent the script to a number of potential partners, including Miramax, Sony and USA Films. Miramax were keen to get involved; Harvey Weinstein phoned Vachon and said 'I love this script. It's fuckin' great. I want to do this movie.'[28] However, there was bad blood between Haynes and Weinstein, as Vachon spells out:

Todd was still smarting from his last Harvey experience. When *Velvet Goldmine* came out, Miramax was behind it in only the most perfunctory way. In Harvey's mind, there was a commercial movie in there but Todd refused to unearth it. From Miramax's perspective, the film got the release it deserved. Todd felt betrayed. So when Harvey calls me to say he wants in on *Far from Heaven*, I'm conflicted [. . .] If I get down on my knees and say to Todd, 'Look, I think we have to do it with Miramax and I will protect you,' he would say OK. But the first time Harvey screwed with the movie (which would've happened), Todd would've blamed me, and I can't put my relationship with Todd in that kind of jeopardy. All this said, in retrospect Miramax may well have been the best distributor for *Far from Heaven*, hands down. Come Oscar time, we would have been everywhere. But the production process would not have been tenable for Todd, and I just knew that.[29]

Miramax were allegedly angry that *Far from Heaven* was going to be made without their support. Indeed, Christine Vachon claims 'that Harvey later said "I'm gonna pay ten million to make sure Julianne Moore does *not* get an Oscar."[30]

Vachon eventually decided to work with USA Films rather than Miramax. This was a risky decision to take. USA Films had been formed in 1999 by Barry Diller following the merger of two independent distributors, Gramercy Pictures and October Films, both of which had affiliations with Universal. Scott Greenstein, formerly a senior figure at Miramax, was the first executive hired at USA Films. The company worked mainly in distribution, with occasional forays into production or co-production. Despite some major successes, however, the profile of the company was questioned by the trade press.[31] Fortunately for Vachon, she had an interlocutor who could assist in her dealings with USA Films: Steven Soderbergh. As she writes,

Steven Soderbergh made *Traffic* with USA Films, and he feels that Scott [Greenstein] got him his Oscar and he's right. Steven heard about *Far from Heaven* at a meeting at CAA long before we even settled the financing. 'Todd Haynes is doing a melodrama? I wanted to do a melodrama', Steven said. We get him a copy of the script and he loves it. Because Steven is a fan of Todd's – and a hugely generous filmmaker – he offers his services as an executive producer to Killer (and brings his buddy George Clooney with him) to help protect Todd from studio pressure. Steven turns out to be our secret weapon.[32]

Soderbergh and Clooney are listed as executive producers in the opening credits of *Far from Heaven*. Whereas Soderbergh's input was fairly considerable, Clooney's was negligible, although his support for the project did help to secure access to finances.

Despite *Far from Heaven* being carefully budgeted, the film still went over its approved costs during filming. The sums of money involved were small by major studio standards – somewhere in the region of $250,000 – but they had not been reported to the companies financing the film. This meant that a bond company had to step in, who tried to find ways to make up for the excess costs: cutting the filming schedule by two days, firing any staff that the film production could do without, and so on. As Haynes recalls,

There was such a negative attitude among the financiers and the bond company – incredible concern, worry and freakout about everything we wanted to do. It made Christine Vachon's job so much harder than it needed to be. It was almost like they were banking on us failing, which is completely unnecessary. It was a weird time at USA Films where there wasn't really a clear leadership, so it was people down below who were making the directives – the pencil pushers. They didn't ever say 'Beautiful dailies, guys', or anything like that. It was just, 'You didn't do this or that.' It was very negative and it made it really tougher than it should have been.[33]

In order to manage the problem with the budget, Vachon had to ask all three of the companies financing *Far from Heaven* – TF1, USA Films and Clear Blue Sky – to pay a third each (between $75,000 and $100,000) of the excess. They all paid up and the bond company retreated.

However, the wranglings of the makers of *Far from Heaven* with their financiers were far from over. Where an independent film financed entirely from the director's own resources, such as *Clerks*, does not really have to satisfy anyone other than the maker, a third of *Far from Heaven*'s budget had been sourced from USA Films, an organisation described by Vachon as 'a new, boutique division of Universal'.[34] Scott Greenstein of USA interfered throughout the film's pre-production and production, and continued to do so after shooting was complete. For instance, USA insisted on test screenings of the finished edit, which Haynes subsequently described as 'a cruel and marginally effective process'.[35] As Vachon recounts the experience:

The testing company Dubin tells us that as a rule of thumb, for an independent film, 'the average' – whatever that means – is about 45 percent of the audience would 'definitely recommend' it to a friend and 25 percent would rank it as 'excellent.' [. . .] At the testing, *Far from Heaven* performs terribly: 8 percent rank it 'excellent' and 13 percent 'definitely recommend' it. Scott Greenstein at USA gets nervous. Audiences couldn't tell if it was a comedy or not. They asked, 'Is this supposed to be funny?'[36]

Around 20 per cent of the test screening audience thought that the film was 'too slow', and so Greenstein asked Haynes to edit the film's length down. Fortunately, as part of the deal that Vachon had made with USA Films, Steven Soderbergh had been given 'final cut' on *Far from Heaven*. Soderbergh thus spent a weekend in Portland with Todd Haynes, scrutinising every cut in the film. However, this did not fully satisfy Greenstein, as Vachon recalls:

By Monday, Todd has taken some of Steven's recommendations for trims and rejected others. More important, Steven completely respects Todd's final decisions and he leaves to go back to work on *Solaris* [2002]. But when Scott at USA hears that Todd didn't take every single one of Steven's ideas, he hints to me that he may not 'support' the film in its release.[37]

Fortunately for Haynes and Vachon, Scott Greenstein was fired just weeks later from his post at USA Films. USA swiftly became a new organisation, Focus Features, and the company's leadership was taken over by Schamus and Linde. Schamus was a supporter of Haynes and his movies, having previously worked with the director. Focus Features became responsible for distributing *Far from Heaven* within the United States, as a title inherited from USA's slate.

Many independent features struggle to attain distribution. If a distribution deal has not been agreed in advance, then the director may attempt to garner support for the work through screenings at film festivals around the world, from Sundance to Cannes, hoping that a distributor will be impressed by the work and offer to pick it up. Vachon had agreed to TF1 distributing *Far from Heaven* in Europe, with USA Films taking care of the same role in the United States. However, this entails relinquishing the movie, and letting the distributors advertise and deliver it to audiences. Vachon feels that Focus Features could have done a better job with Haynes's film:

As the head of Focus Features, James [Schamus] was responsible for distributing and promoting *Far from Heaven*. We opened the movie in the late fall of 2002, and by late winter – Oscar time – it had made $15 million. *The Pianist* [Polanski, 2002], the other Oscar contender from Focus, opened a little later and made nearly double that. When our movie was overlooked at the Golden Globes and the Oscars – *The Pianist* took home multiple awards – as the producer, I wanted to blame Focus. Couldn't they have pushed it a little harder?[38]

Of course, this concern – that a distributor could have done more to 'push' a particular film on its slate – could be raised by producers of individual films of all sizes, from low-budget indie to mainstream blockbuster. And Focus helped *Far from Heaven* to reach a large enough domestic audience for it to take more at the box office (almost $16 million) than it cost to make. (The film also took more than $13 million overseas, making for a worldwide box office performance of just over $29 million.) However, what Vachon's comment does reveal is the complex tangle of financial support, 'artistic' status and clout, awards potential and box office draw that the muddled field of 'independent' cinema in the United States can now involve.

Casting

The most significant roles in *Far from Heaven* – Cathy (Julianne Moore), Raymond (Dennis Haysbert) and Frank (Dennis Quaid) – are all played by actors familiar to a significant percentage of audiences. All three had appeared in dozens of films before appearing in *Far from Heaven*; all three had extensive experience of working in mainstream American cinema. Their casting in Haynes's film somewhat complicates its categorisation as an 'independent' title. Indie cinema has often been marked by its use of relative unknowns – as with, for instance, *The Blair Witch Project* (Myrick and Sánchez, 1999), *In Search of a Midnight Kiss* (Holdridge, 2007) or any of the 'Mumblecore' movies – or by its casting of actors known for working almost exclusively outside of the mainstream, such as Parker Posey. However, the casting of Moore, Haysbert and Quaid exposes some of the complexities that have come into play as the boundaries between major studio, mini-major, classics division and major independent, and 'true' independent have become blurred.

Todd Haynes had written the script for *Far from Heaven* with Julianne Moore in mind for the role of Cathy. He had previously worked with her on *Safe*, a hybrid melodrama/horror film in which Moore plays Carol White, a woman who develops 'environmental illness' and leaves her family behind to live in a desert retreat. In returning to melodrama, and a narrative centred on a woman who suffers, Haynes knew that Moore would excel in the role (and that the two of them could work productively together). Rather than going through her agent, Haynes sent the script directly to Moore. As she recalls,

> He completely took me by surprise when he called me one day and told me that he had written this script. And I'd honestly thought that he was just calling to say hello. And we were chatting, and then finally, he said, 'I wrote a movie, for you.' And he said, 'Should I send it?' I was like, 'Are you kidding?' So he over-nighted it and I got it on a Saturday and I read it on the subway to the gym. And the only person I could talk to about it was the person I was working out with, my trainer. I was so excited – 'Oh, I'm in this movie!' – and she could care less. She was like, 'Lift it again.'[39]

Impressed by the *Far from Heaven* script, she signed on swiftly.

Julianne Moore has, throughout her career, oscillated between the mainstream film industry and independent movies. There are more of the latter on her CV, and it is arguable that she takes the mainstream roles merely in order to pay the rent. (This is supported by the fact that her husband is Bart Freundlich, who has made the indie films *The Myth of Fingerprints* (1997), *World Traveler* (2001) and *Trust the Man* (2006) – though he has also written and directed more mainstream fare, including the romantic comedy *The Rebound* (2009).) Moore's indie cachet is related in significant part to her roles in films for celebrated auteurs such as Robert Altman (*Short Cuts*, 1993; *Cookie's Fortune*, 1999), Paul Thomas Anderson (*Boogie Nights*, 1997; *Magnolia*, 1999) and the Coen brothers (*The Big Lebowski*, 1998). She also has queer indie credentials: in addition to her films with Haynes, she has worked with Gus Van Sant (*Psycho*, 1998), Tom Kalin (*Savage Grace*, 2007) and Tom Ford (*A Single Man*, 2009), and has played lesbian roles in *The Hours* (Daldry, 2002) and *The Kids Are All Right* (Cholodenko, 2010). Indeed, she was awarded an 'excellence in media' award in 2004 by GLAAD (the Gay and Lesbian Alliance Against Defamation). However, Moore's mainstream work – which includes *The Fugitive* (Davis, 1993), *Nine Months* (Columbus, 1995), *The Lost World: Jurassic Park* (Spielberg, 1997), *Evolution* (Reitman, 2001), *The Forgotten* (Ruben, 2004) and *Next* (Tamahori, 2007) – has helped to provide her with a level of public and commercial visibility that many actors struggle to attain. This visibility is also enhanced through her modelling work, and celebrity endorsement of Revlon and Bulgari.

Julianne Moore serves as a valuable index of the shifting nature of 'independent' cinema in the United States. Her ability to move between the different areas of production registers the crumbling of the distinctions between them. As Diane Negra has noted, in an essay on Parker Posey, there are

star characteristics and cultural conditions which make some performers eligible for 'cross over' from the category of independent to big-budget filmmaking while restricting others. Not only have performers as varied as Anne Heche, Billy Bob Thornton, Ashley Judd, Matthew McConnaughey, and Renee Zellwegger crossed over from independent film into big budget filmmaking, but it is becoming increasingly common to 'commute' between the two realms as the industrial and economic lines between them become increasingly difficult to draw. Consequently, independent film has emerged as a productive site for Hollywood stars to either accumulate artistic capital (Tori Spelling), pursue uncommercial vanity projects (Al Pacino) or rehabilitate waning stardom (John Travolta, Marisa Tomei).[40]

If the capacity to 'commute' between independent and bigger-budget films requires certain 'star characteristics', then what is it about Julianne Moore (and, perhaps, other actors) that enables her to move so freely? Moore, arguably, is a malleable performer who has not become associated with one specific role or character type. She is often praised and admired for her acting versatility and for her risk-taking (as with, for instance, her scenes in *Short Cuts*). Further, unlike many stars, she mostly manages to keep her private life out of the media. This is not to say that she avoids publicising her films, or shuns party invitations, but that she manages to frame her domestic life of husband and children as routine, conventional, banal, and her working life as 'just a job', albeit one to which she is seriously committed. Consequently, her appearances in tabloids and in gossip magazines are negligible.

The casting of Moore brought its own financial and pragmatic hurdles for *Far from Heaven*. Moore's career was going well in 2001; when pre-production of Haynes's film began, she was shooting the *Silence of the Lambs* sequel *Hannibal* in Italy with director Ridley Scott, and her salary asking price had risen to around $5 million per film. However, due to her proclivity for working on both mainstream and lower-budgeted indie fare, producer Christine Vachon was able to negotiate a much lower fee – six figures, rather than seven – with Moore's agent. Despite this, Moore's attachment to the project affected the film's budget in other ways. Haynes and Vachon had initially wanted to film in Toronto. Many US films and television programmes are shot in Canada, where tax incentives help to keep shooting costs down. However, Moore insisted on filming in New York, so that she could be near her family. This raised the budget of the film from $12 million to almost $14 million, meaning that Vachon had to raise additional financing before shooting could begin. Moore also delivered a further complexity: mid-August, two months before filming started, she revealed to Vachon that she was pregnant. The shoot went ahead. Moore's waistline expanded from 26 inches to 36 inches during the filming, necessitating regular reshaping of individual costumes. Reflecting on this complication later, Vachon suggested that it worked in the film's favour: 'Normally she is incredibly slim and her face is very striking, but with a little bit of pregnancy weight, she looks much softer and more 1950s.'[41]

Casting Frank, Cathy's husband, was more difficult. Haynes wrote the part with James Gandolfini in mind, but the flexibility of the actor's schedule was severely restricted by his work on the HBO television series

The Sopranos (1999–2007). The second choice was Russell Crowe, who allegedly said, after reading the script, 'Fuck, I'd play Cathy, but why would I want to play this guy? He's not even the lead.'[42] This became a problem for Haynes and Vachon as they searched for an actor. As Vachon puts it in her account of the film's production, 'Cathy is the man's part, and Frank, the husband, is the woman's part. Every male actor we send the script to wants to know if he's missing some pages from the script.'[43] After Crowe, the third choice was Jeff Bridges. Haynes met with him in Santa Barbara, and entertained some of the actor's ideas about potential alterations to the script, but Killer Films could not meet Bridges's salary expectations.[44]

Other names were suggested as possibilities. Scott Greenstein of USA Films proposed Greg Kinnear and Hugh Jackman. But then *Far from Heaven*'s casting director Laura Rosenthal saw Dennis Quaid in Norman Jewison's television movie *Dinner with Friends* (2001), and at around the same time Quaid's agent, George Freeman, suggested his name to Vachon. Haynes watched some of Quaid's films in order to consider him, and could see the actor working in the role. As Vachon reflects,

Todd really goes for Dennis. And it turns out that Dennis is a huge *Velvet Goldmine* fan. All George had to do is *mention* it, and Dennis is in. Except Dennis hasn't really done low-budget movies. I was afraid he was going to show up, see his trailer, and say, 'what the fuck is this?' As it turned out, he loved shooting a lower-budget film since he was used to sitting in his trailer and waiting and waiting. Comparatively, for Dennis, working on *Far from Heaven* must have felt like being in the Green Berets.[45]

This comment reveals the significance of casting Quaid in a film with such a low budget. For most of his career, the actor has enjoyed leading man status in films from *The Big Easy* (McBride, 1986), *Innerspace* (Dante, 1987) and *Great Balls of Fire!* (McBride, 1989) to *Frequency* (Hoblit, 2000) and *Pandorum* (Alvart, 2009). At the peak of his popularity in the 1980s, Quaid was romantically connected to Meg Ryan. Vachon saw that this could work in *Far from Heaven*'s favour: 'When Dennis Quaid married Meg Ryan, she was America's sweetheart, and he was the male equivalent. They *were* Cathy and Frank.'[46]

Quaid's presence in *Far from Heaven*, then, engages with a recognisable indie cinema strategy: that of casting a well-known actor against type. Independent cinema operates as a sphere of production in which, for a significantly smaller fee, an actor can work with up-and-coming talent, and demonstrate their versatility and acting ability by breaking with their established star identity. They can also boost their standing as an individual who (at least seems to) value the skill and craft of acting over financial reward, and who will accept a less glamorous role, perhaps even as part of an ensemble cast. Other examples of this casting strategy in recent indie cinema would include Tom Cruise's role as a sleazy motivational speaker in *Magnolia*, Robin Williams's creepy retail photo clerk in *One Hour Photo* (Romanek, 2002) and Charlize Theron's portrayal of serial killer Aileen Wuornos in *Monster* (Jenkins, 2003). The desire of actors to play such roles has had a significant influence on the blurring of the distinction between independent cinema and the output of the major studios; as Geoff King notes, 'Pressure resulting from the desire of stars to work with a new generation of filmmakers is . . . one of the factors that drew the majors towards the indie sector in the second half of the 1990s.'[47]

Dennis Haysbert was cast in the third key role in *Far from Heaven*, as gardener Raymond Deagan. Haysbert had an extensive and varied history of working in film and television, with roles in mainstream films including *Love Field* (Kaplan, 1992), *Waiting to Exhale* (Whitaker, 1995) and *Random Hearts* (Pollack, 1999). He also had experience of the lower-budgeted independent, however, having worked on titles including *Suture* (McGehee and Siegel, 1993) and *The Minus Man* (Fancher, 1999). At the same time that *Far from Heaven* was shooting, Haysbert was involved in making the first season of the Fox television series *24*, which premiered in the United States in November 2001. As *24* was shooting in Los Angeles and *Far from Heaven* in New York State, Haysbert spent considerable time flying between coasts during the film's production.

Other, more minor roles in the cast of *Far from Heaven* may also mark the film as 'independent' to those familiar with the terrain. Patricia Clarkson was cast as Cathy's best friend, Eleanor Fine. Although she has appeared in the occasional big-budget studio film (*Jumanji* (Johnston, 1995); *The Green Mile* (Darabont, 1999)), Clarkson is best known for her roles in a raft of independent movies, including *High Art* (Cholodenko, 1998), *All the Real Girls* (Green, 2003), *Dogville* (von Trier, 2003) and *Good Night, and Good Luck* (Clooney, 2005). Other 'indie' faces that appear in the film include Michael Gaston, who plays Eleanor's husband Stan, Celia Weston, cast as town gossip Mona Lauder, and Matt Malloy, who makes a brief appearance mid-way through the film as a red-faced man at the Whitakers' annual party. American independent cinema often draws on the same – admittedly fairly substantial – pool of acting talent. The actors in this pool can gain credibility and cachet for appearing in such films; the movies themselves become marked as 'indie' due to their casting choices.

Acting

In addition to budget and casting as markers of independence, acting and performance style can also be used to identify a film as operating outside of the mainstream. Big-budget, studio-produced cinema's conventions for acting often operate as the 'norm' against which independent cinema purposefully differentiates itself. In doing so, independent productions may be pointedly exposing the artifice of performance that Hollywood style attempts to deny or conceal behind editing, musical score, and so on. Alternatively, they may be offering up a different style of acting for audiences to enjoy, one that might be notably more raw, 'authentic' or challenging to view. As Andrew Higson has argued, in relation to more experimental and avant-garde forms of independent cinema, the acting style in such films may be purposefully marked by 'unconventional vocal strategies' and 'stylised and mannered performance', whether minimalist or excessive.[48]

Acting in independent cinema is affected by a range of different factors, including the experience of the cast and director, the budget, the training and rehearsal time offered to the actors, the intentions of the filmmakers, and so on. A large number of independent films have used amateur actors or family and friends in many or all of their roles, perhaps reserving those with some minor experience for the lead roles. This has the benefit of keeping costs low, but it can challenge the audience to accept a cast acting in an alternative register. The tricks and training used by actors and stars working in the mainstream to make their characters believable, and maybe empathetic, may be lacking; delivery of lines may be stilted, the ability to modulate the voice not as delicate, the expressivity of the face and body not as carefully nuanced (if at all). For example, for the first decade of his career, from *Hag in a Black Leather Jacket* (1964) to *Desperate Living* (1977), John Waters largely used his friends and allies in his movies, with some of the 'actors' (Divine, Edith Massey, Mink Stole) appearing in film after film. Although Divine was able to offer some variety in emotional register, could deliver lines in a range of tones, and was adept at striking poses and a certain sort of physical comedy, her campy performance style (entirely in keeping with her drag persona) was cartoonish and often exaggerated. In contrast, Edith Massey has a distinctive vocal sound, abrasive and harsh, but her facial expression rarely changes. As Waters writes of Massey,

> She worried about memorizing lines but solved the problem by writing her dialogue over and over until she knew it by heart [. . .] Sometimes she had studied the script so meticulously that she would include the written direction in her reading: 'Oh yes, Officer, I've got your money for you. Edith reaches in pocket and gives cop a bill.' I would explain that the words in parentheses were not part of her dialogue.[49]

Inconsistency in acting style is often on display in the independent films that rely on amateur actors, as a film such as Kevin Smith's *Clerks*, discussed previously, or many of the films by Bruce LaBruce (*No Skin Off My Ass*, 1991; *Super 8½*, 1995; *Hustler White*, 1996; *The Raspberry Reich*, 2004) demonstrate. For some audiences, 'bad acting' can provide its own pleasures, whether for the unintentional hilarity it may cause, or for the alternative it provides to Hollywood slickness.

One significant aspect of independent cinema in relation to performance is that directors can sometimes utilise filming methodologies and tactics that would usually be encumbered by the protocols of major-budget production. Total shooting time is likely to be much shorter, the time between takes and set-ups will probably be abbreviated, there will be fewer crew members, and the number of different locations may be much smaller. There may also be the opportunity to experiment with filming scenes in ways that would not be available to mainstream directors who need to work within the formal codes of the studio film. Geoff King discusses the example of Richard Linklater's film *Tape* (2001), which

> was thoroughly rehearsed in advance before being shot on two digital cameras with little advance blocking of sequences. The performers worked their way through the script in ten-minute chunks, each of which was covered four or five times. The visual style of the film includes dialogue exchanges at several key moments rendered in repeated fast pans from one character to another, a device that maintains the real-time existence of the interaction between performers, for up to four minutes unbroken in one case.[50]

In this example, then, the speed of production, in addition to the use of specific filming technologies which facilitate a more immersive experience for the actors, had an impact on the style of performance adopted. King also discusses the films of John Cassavetes, and the techniques that he used in order to elicit certain types of performances from his cast:

The pro-filmic reality that matters in the films of John Cassavetes ... the 'reality' to be documented by the camera, is that of the unfolding performance of actors and the emotional reality of character to which it aspires. To respect this as much as possible ... Cassavetes favoured long takes, shot in real time with a combination of close, hand-held camerawork and more distanced telephoto coverage from a second camera [. . .] Vast amounts of footage were expended in the effort to capture the right moment ... Much was also shot in sequence, to create emotional coherence and continuity of a kind closer to that found in theatre than the usual practice in film.[51]

The final outcome of these processes – in films such as *Faces* (1968) – is a notable intensity of performance from the cast members. Other independent directors have also used long takes in order to enable actors to immerse themselves fully in their characters. David Lynch's *Inland Empire* (2006), for instance, features a monologue delivered by Laura Dern direct to camera that is unedited and lasts for several minutes; David Gordon Green's films, such as *All the Real Girls*, often employ this technique.

In other cases, independent film allows actors, whether amateur or trained, to experiment with performance styles. Improvisation is a constituent component of many of the narrative films of Andy Warhol, for instance, such as *Horse* (1965), *Chelsea Girls* (1966) or *Bike Boy* (1967). Before his mostly static camera, actors in these films have rambling, free-form conversations and attempt to coerce each other into particular activities (sex, a meal, a haircut). Whereas improvisation is perhaps more commonly associated with theatre, live comedy and certain forms of music such as jazz, utilising this practice with film provides the completed work with a particular distinctive character. Of course, mainstream films (especially in the genre of comedy) may allow some room for their cast to improvise around scenes and script, but on the whole this is a limited practice. In a further raft of independent films, alternative modes of acting are attempted. In the movies of Hal Hartley, for instance, which include *The Unbelievable Truth* (1989), *Trust* (1990) and *Simple Men* (1992), the mannered scripts are intoned by the actors in a largely affectless manner, even when the plot elements are dramatic or emotionally charged. This formal challenge to mainstream codes requires audiences to recognise how the conventional handling of script and dialogue is merely one of many possible options.

In the case of *Far from Heaven*, as a constituent component of his homage to Douglas Sirk's melodramas, Haynes was interested in reviving a style of performance that was no longer used. During the 1950s, when Sirk was making the movies that served as the main inspiration for Haynes's film, the acting style he favoured was competing with a growth of interest in Method acting, the latter used by James Dean, Marlon Brando, Montgomery Clift and others. Method acting emphasises the importance of character interiority and psychology, and (especially in the form advocated by Lee Strasberg of the Actors Studio, arguably its most famous tutor) refers to the practice by which actors draw on their own emotions and memories in bringing a character to life. The acting style adopted in Sirk's cinema was markedly different to this. As Haynes comments,

It is such a *big* acting style. But it's not exactly ironic; there's no winking, no being superior to the text, and there's also no infusing the text with this idea of an innate psychological depth, which is what the Method idea of acting is about. Instead it's about excavation. There's usually something the characters are discovering about themselves, but these characters don't articulate what they learn, and accordingly the dialogue is very much about surface. Everything is on the surface in a way that is not actually comforting in our society today, which is so much defined by psychology.[52]

Taking this as a basis, Haynes developed a script that would have an impact on the performance style adopted by his cast:

We set up a very specific series of restraints in approaching this film, and it began with the writing. It was as if there was only a certain number of words that could be spoken, a certain series of phrases, certain gestures that could take place – and nothing beyond that. It's in a way that still feels like stock dialogue.[53]

Haynes suggests that the style of acting such a script provokes from actors is 'just a little bit more heightened, a little bit cleaner and tidier than today's more Method-infused naturalism'.[54] Julianne Moore has talked about performing in this manner: 'There's a great deal of artifice to the style, but in a sense it's actually quite easy to do, because this genre of film is something that we're very familiar with.'[55]

Moore's acting, in particular, gained significant critical plaudits. As was noted in the Introduction, she won awards at the Venice Film

Festival in 2002 for her performance, and was nominated for a Golden Globe and an Academy Award. Manohla Dargis, in her review of the film for the *Los Angeles Times*, wrote that

The film's three leads are extraordinary, but what Moore does with her role is so beyond the parameters of what we call great acting that it nearly defies categorisation. Although it's the least naturalistic of the performances because the character is an artificial construction, yet another imitation of life, it's also the most devastating.[56]

As Geoffrey O'Brien comments of Moore's performance, neatly capturing the specific acting style in *Far from Heaven*, 'She plays her part as someone who reads the lines she's been given as if she senses their falseness but can't come up with an alternative.'[57] In relation to the arguments of this chapter, the notable aspect of the performances in *Far from Heaven* is that they are in a register distant from conventional norms – historically outmoded, recognisable but artificial, distinct from present-day codes of mainstream cinema – and yet the artistry and the skill of the film's cast was repeatedly identified and praised by critics.

Visual Style

One further aspect that often sets independent films apart from those produced by the mainstream is that they adopt a different look. Whilst movies made by mainstream studios also offer a broad array of visual styles, independent films can mark their difference by (for example) using a colour palette that is wilfully experimental and 'artistic', even pointedly 'unrealistic'. In drawing attention to their visual form, such films can place a barrier between the audience and their immersion in the narrative; at the same time, they can invite a type of appreciation and spectatorial pleasure that the mainstream – with its dominant codes of realism – regularly bypasses. Certainly, as the field of independent production has blurred with that of the major studios, this distinction has been somewhat undermined. As Yannis Tzioumakis notes, for instance, three of Wes Anderson's films – *Rushmore* (1998), *The Royal Tennenbaums* (2001), *The Life Aquatic with Steve Zissou* (2004), all with distinctive visual styles that may seem to mark them as 'indie' – were co-financed and distributed by Disney.[58] However, it remains the case that independent cinema, whether it is made within or outside of the orbit of the major studios, often distinguishes itself from mainstream fare through an innovative employment of visual aesthetic strategies and devices.

Many indie movies produced over the last few decades, for example, have marked their independence by filming in black and white: *Eraserhead*, *She's Gotta Have It* (Lee, 1986), *Swoon*, *Go Fish*, *Clerks*, *Pi* (Aronofsky, 1998), *The Man Who Wasn't There* (Coen, 2001). Shooting with black and white film stock carries connotations of 'artistry' which separates such films from the commercial mainstream, irrespective of how generic or amateurish the content of the completed project. Mainstream films only very occasionally use black and white; in recent decades, studio films have utilised the palette for historical tales (Spielberg's *Schindler's List* [1993]) and comic book adaptations (*Sin City* [Miller/Rodriguez, 2005]). For the indie director, black and white can also assist in forging intimate access to the film's characters, even to the point of claustrophobia, perhaps due to an association between black and white footage and smaller, more democratically accessible (that is, 'home movie') cameras. Thus, the cramped apartments used as locations in *Eraserhead* and *Pi* are rendered more unsettling due to their being shot in black and white.

In many other instances, independent directors utilise visual styles that are distant from codes of realism, and that clearly mark their movies as fictional constructs. Gregg Araki's films *The Doom Generation* (1995) and *Nowhere* (1997), for instance, both feature brightly coloured set design that is patently artificial: extravagant murals, walls painted to match characters' clothing, a motel room in which every surface and object is decorated in black and white squares (see Figure 1). In these films, this excessive look fits with the dialogue; the youthful characters mostly speak in a hyperbolic form of adolescent lingo. The visual style is also an effective and economically savvy way of marking the films as distinct; the sets used were not expensive to create, and provided striking images that could be used as publicity materials. As a second example, Richard Linklater's films *Waking Life* (2001) and his Philip K. Dick adaptation, *A Scanner Darkly* (2006), both utilised digital rotoscoping techniques, in which standard filmed footage was subsequently manipulated using animator Bob Rabiston's Rotoshop software (see Figure 2). The resulting movies – in which actors become cartoons of themselves, and aspects of the set and lines of dialogue can be enabled to have a life of their own – were the first feature-length titles to use the software.

Other independent movies may contain striking visual moments which, through their deployment by marketing and advertising strategies

Figure 1 Gregg Araki's *Nowhere* (© Kill)

Figure 2 Richard Linklater's *Waking Life* (© Twentieth Century Fox Film Corporation)

(stills, trailers) and their isolation from the movie by cultural commentators and audience memory, can mark the films as 'artistic', and their directors as creative and inventive. Indie films which have benefited from incorporating such moments include *Reservoir Dogs*, *Donnie Darko* (Kelly, 2001), *Mulholland Drive* (Lynch, 2001), *Garden State* (Braff, 2004) and *The Fall* (Singh, 2006). Of course, many big-budget mainstream films are also sold to audiences via images and trailers that promise a combination of ingenuity and spectacle, through strategically selected moments; in the case of independent films, such tactics reveal that it is not necessary to spend millions of dollars to create memorable and innovative cinema.

In relation to *Far from Heaven*, the film's distinct recreation of Sirk's visual style was on display in the still images and trailer used to market the film; it was also discussed in detail by Haynes in interviews. Although the trailer did not fully recreate the overblown, hectic rush of many of the original trailers for 1950s melodramas, in which slogans would be dashed across the screen as a lead actress buried her face in a duvet or a man's shoulder, the tag line used for *Far from Heaven* – 'what imprisons desires of the heart?' – echoed that format. Significantly, the visual style of Haynes's film, in reviving a look associated with one particular director, was a rarity in the cinema of the early 2000s – as it had been for decades, and continues to be now.

The look of Haynes's film was meticulously put together through a combination of set design, costume design, props, lighting and cinematography. Haynes and his collaborators studied the films of Douglas Sirk closely, paying particular attention to his choices of objects, textures and colours. Haynes has noted the difference between Sirk's uses of colour and that of many other directors:

Today's use of colour is totally reductive. Happy scenes are warm, sad scenes are cool; sometimes an entire movie, if it's set in the past, will be shot through honey-coloured gels. The Woody Allen period films are just gilded gold, warm butterscotch. What's beautiful about Sirk is that every frame is a complementary palette. Every single scene, regardless if it's happy or sad, plays with an interaction of warm and cool colours. It's so powerful.[59]

Having identified this variety at work in Sirk, Haynes went through his script and planned colours for individual locations and sequences, creating very detailed colour charts for almost every scene: 'I would sit down, close my eyes, think of a scene, and go through swatches and put together a range of colours that communicated a mood.'[60] These colour charts were then presented to the set and costume designers as guidance for putting together the individual components of the film's look.

In creating these colour charts, Haynes was returning to a system of production design used by the Hollywood studios in earlier decades, known as 'colour scoring'. This system, as Scott Higgins notes, 'was born during the era of Technicolor and . . . reached baroque heights in the 1950s'.[61] He continues:

Haynes' method of developing a palette for the film during the early stages of pre-production runs parallel to the work of the Technicolor colour consultants who mapped out colour designs based on the continuity script. The Color Advisory Service, under the guidance of Natalie Kalmus, assured Technicolor a degree of aesthetic control over virtually every colour feature produced in Hollywood from the 1930s through to the early 1950s. The colour consultants' aim was a polished and harmonised colour design carefully wrought to support dramatic turning points and closely monitored to avoid distracting accents. The Color Advisory Service was largely responsible for the determined sense of colour, the pervading feeling of order and precision, in many classical Hollywood productions.[62]

The model texts from which Haynes and his team drew their inspiration, however, were largely made at the tail end of this period. Films by Nicholas Ray, Douglas Sirk and Vincente Minnelli pushed the limits of colour scoring and the effects that it could have. As Higgins notes of these three directors,

Working at the very end of Technicolor's reign and at the beginning of Eastmancolor, their films tend to exaggerate colour scoring conventions and bring them to decorative designs [. . .] Scholars and critics often attribute the invention of this style to Sirk, but his production team was working within, and extrapolating from, an established tradition of colour melodrama.[63]

In relation to *Far from Heaven*, Haynes was determined that the production team should push Sirk's exaggerated version of colour scoring even further. As he has acknowledged,

I said at one point, 'I just don't want to feel like the Sirk films were bolder than we were. Let's go man, let's take it as an invitation, to really try stuff that most people are afraid to try, it doesn't seem naturalistic. There's no logical source of the lights, of the colours, you can't explain it naturalistically or architecturally. Let's let the music swell here, let's really push it.'[64]

In addition to his colour charts, Haynes also put together a large source book of images for inspiration in creating the style of the film, which included paintings, photographs, stills from movies, and adverts and magazine spreads from the 1950s. In some cases, individual images served as an influence on particular moments in the film. A turquoise tablecloth in the Whitakers' home, visible in the party sequence, was lifted directly from a *Life* magazine spread. When Frank visits the

Ritz cinema, a shot of him lurking at the back of the auditorium contains a reference to Edward Hopper's painting *New York Movie* (1939). And – as will be discussed in detail in the next chapter's exploration of authorship – moments from a range of specific movies were also quoted or referenced during the creation of *Far from Heaven*'s look. When Julianne Moore lies sobbing across her bed near the film's conclusion, for instance, the framing is borrowed directly from a similar scene in *The Reckless Moment* (Ophüls, 1949).

The artificial, heightened nature of the visual style of *Far from Heaven* extended to every aspect of the production design. As Haynes has stated, the look of the film was based primarily on movies of the 1950s, not on the actual 1950s.[65] Mark Friedberg, the film's production designer, has talked about building the set of the Whitakers' house: 'Todd wanted us to build a set that looked like a set. Most of what you do in my job is try to make sets that don't look like you built them. You try to design yourself out of the story so then it feels "normal".'[66] Haynes extended this 'fakeness' to exterior locations:

I wanted every car perfectly polished and clean. We had to take gritty New Jersey exterior locations and clean them up. We had buildings cleaned because they had birdshit hanging off the edge or they had too much dirt, and we had to make it look as much like a back-lot soundstage as possible.[67]

This 'movie' look reaches its apotheosis in *Far from Heaven* in a short sequence of Cathy driving in her car, just after she has been doorstepped by representatives of the NAACP (National Association for the Advancement of Colored People). The back projection that screens behind her is actually the original plates from Sirk's *Written on the Wind*. This blatantly fake rear projection work – not unlike that in Tarantino's *Pulp Fiction* – contributes to the film's distinctive visual style, and marks it as a fabrication.

Political Content

Mainstream Hollywood cinema has always had a tendency to provide diverting and distracting entertainment, and not to engage directly with real-world politics; it also favours concentrating on certain types of characters (white, heterosexual, relatively affluent), and telling stories that wrap up neatly and positively in the closing minutes. For those filmmakers who want to redress the balance – to feature non-white, non-heterosexual or working-class characters; leave their stories open-ended or with a downbeat conclusion; directly confront specific political topics – then working independently might be a necessity. Independent American cinema has often been associated with markedly political content, from the jazz-inflected depictions of black life in the films of Shirley Clarke (such as *The Cool World*, 1964) to Sadie Benning's pixel-vision accounts of her teenage dyke existence (including *Me and Rubyfruit*, 1989, and *Jollies*, 1990).

The association between independent cinema and the political is evident even from the titles of books on this area of film production. Donald Lyons's text is called *Independent Visions*; Emanuel Levy's is titled *Cinema of Outsiders*.[68] The independent sector, these books both suggest, enables directors with particular challenging points of view the possibility of expressing themselves without hindrance or interference. As Geoff King writes,

An important aspect of any definition of independent cinema . . . is the space it offers – potentially, at least – for the expression of alternative social, political and/or ideological perspectives [. . .] The American indie sector has . . . provided an arena hospitable to a number of constituencies generally subjected to neglect or stereotypical representation in the mainstream, the most prominent cases in recent decades being black- and gay-oriented cinema. Greater scope has been found for more liberal, open or radical treatment of contentious issues . . ., freed to a significant extent from the relatively narrow moral economy typically operative in Hollywood. Independent features have in many cases been able to avoid the kind of ideologically loaded imaginary reconciliations used in Hollywood features to smooth away any awkward social or political issues that might initially be confronted.[69]

Of course, as King acknowledges, this is not to say that the indie sector cannot produce films as conservative and formally homogeneous as those produced by the major studios. However, one factor that may affect the decision by a director to make a film independently may be the potential to give voice to a neglected viewpoint.

Far from Heaven, as has already been acknowledged, sits in the grey area between studio picture and independent film. Partly supported in its production finances by USA Films, and distributed by Focus Features, the film is thus connected to a major studio, Universal. How politically challenging, then, can its content be? Certainly, when considered formally and ideologically, *Far from Heaven* does not initially seem as complex or challenging as Haynes's other films. It adopts – or mimics – the form of classical Hollywood melodrama of the 1950s, from musical score to camera movement. The varied and intercut styles of *Poison* (black and white horror film, period prison drama, documentary) and lengthy, often static takes of *Safe* are notably absent. In addition, some of the explicit and contentious content of Haynes's earlier films – the rough sex between the prisoners in *Poison*, for example – is not on display. And yet one of the main intentions behind making *Far from Heaven*, it would seem, was to re-insert the political content that was often missing, or only obliquely referred to, in Sirk's original films. This is not to say, of course, that Sirk's films did not address particular political concerns. In *All That Heaven Allows*, middle-class widow Cary (Jane Wyman) has to overcome resistance to her burgeoning relationship with her working-class gardener Ron (Rock Hudson). *Imitation of Life* features racial concerns within its plot – specifically, the hopes of Annie (Juanita Moore) that her 'mulatta' daughter, Sarah Jane (Susan Kohlner), will accept her black identity. But *Far from Heaven* reworks Cary and Ron's relationship into one that crosses the boundaries of race, and Frank's grappling with his homosexuality (through visits to bars, surreptitious liaisons and trips to a psychiatrist) introduces a topic – queerness – entirely absent from Sirk's œuvre. As Sharon Willis observes of *Far from Heaven*'s politics,

Because Haynes's film elaborates on the social pressures that Sirk's films, like their historical milieu, repressed, marginalised, or 'euphemized', we could describe its project as both archaeological and fantasy-driven: archaeological because it seeks to restore the social subtext whose anxieties the films captured in their exquisitely overwrought dramas and décors; fantasy-driven because *Far from Heaven* lavishes an obsessive attention upon moments when the 1950s 'unspeakables', the loves that dare not speak their names, homosexuality and interracial sex, body forth in all their scandalous effects.[70]

Certainly, the fact that homosexuality features centrally in the plot of *Far from Heaven* can be understood as a strategy of fantastic re-imagining. Rock Hudson played the male romantic lead in several of Sirk's films. Although Sirk knew that Hudson was gay, he assisted in the construction of the actor's rugged masculine persona. As Barbara Klinger has noted, when viewed retrospectively these films can seem camp, with individual lines suggesting queer innuendo that was (most likely) unintended at the time.[71] Haynes parlays audience knowledge about Hudson's real identity, and the camp appreciation of Sirk's films, into Frank's plotline.

The content of *Far from Heaven* may not seem that shocking or scandalous to a contemporary audience. As noted in the Introduction, although the original version of the script had Cathy walking in on Frank giving another man a blowjob in his office, this was changed to her catching the two men kissing – which ultimately had an effect on the film's classification. In the US, the film was given a PG-13 rating, for one use of the word 'fuck'. This occurs as Cathy and Frank are leaving the office of the psychiatrist to whom Frank confesses his homosexual urges. Though Cathy tries to be supportive, Frank snaps '*Look!* I just want to get the whole *fucking* thing over with! Can you understand that?' As a break with the meticulously maintained Sirkian style, this line provides a moment of surprising rupture. It also, in retrospect, can be read as a witty comment on the sexual relationship between Frank and Cathy, and Frank's wish to avoid having sex ('the whole *fucking* thing') with his wife.

What is especially notable about the politics of *Far from Heaven* is the attention the film bestows on three particular characters who are all in positions of disenfranchisement or disempowerment. That is to say, Cathy is a middle-class mother in a sham marriage, Raymond is an educated black man whose knowledge and refinement have not quite enabled him to escape from working as a gardener (his plant shop, he says, is 'the only thing that business degree's been good for yet'), and Frank is a homosexual desperate to find release and love with another man. *Far from Heaven* does not posit these three characters as equal – though they are lined up in the publicity poster for the film in a manner that suggests audiences should consider their respective significance and status. In her review of the film, Laura Mulvey notes the film's exploration of cross-race relationships, and homosexuality:

At first, *Far from Heaven* might seem to suggest that these two social oppressions are equal and parallel in intensity, but as the plot unfolds social anxiety at homosexuality is shown to be infinitely less deep rooted than the hysteria caused by intimacy across the racial divide. Cathy and Raymond's friendship touches an absolute taboo in Hartford, Connecticut. While gayness may be persecuted by law, Haynes suggests that Frank might well find not only happiness with his lover but also a new form of friendship with Cathy and the children.[72]

I will return to this topic, of the film's handling of concerns related to gender, sexuality and race, in subsequent chapters of this book. In Chapter 3, I will demonstrate how they are intimately connected to Haynes's resuscitation and reworking of melodrama as a genre, and in Chapter 4, I will argue that *Far from Heaven*'s 'queerness' extends far beyond Frank's plotline.

Conclusion

This chapter has provided an overview of particular ways in which *Far from Heaven* can be framed as an independent film, and the challenges it poses to such a categorisation. Space has been devoted to exploring the contemporary landscape of independent film production in the United States, and the ways in which the field has altered since the 1980s. In addition, consideration has been given to *Far from Heaven*'s budget and financing, its casting, the acting style adopted for the film, the visual style used, and the movie's politics in relation to gender, sexuality and race. Despite some elements of the film – the casting of 'stars', the lush orchestral score – seeming to mark the film as 'mainstream', this chapter has examined the ways in which the film fits with critical and practical understandings of independent production, and how it troubles those conceptualisations.

2. Authorship

Independent cinema is often identified as a realm of production in which directors can have (near to) full control over their own material. In practical terms, this may involve taking on several different roles which, on a big-budget film, would be divided up amongst a team of contributors: writing the script, directing, acting, editing, composing the soundtrack. (On the independent horror film *Paranormal Activity* (2007), for instance, Oren Peli served as the film's writer, director, producer, editor and cinematographer, and used his own house as the main shooting location.) Along with the smaller crew working on any independent film, the director can arguably steer his or her creative vision more successfully when they have a hand in multiple aspects of the production. This can lead to an understanding of independent cinema as a field dominated by the singular visions of multi-tasking mavericks. As Geoff Andrew writes, for instance,

The history of the American cinema is littered with free spirits who, rather than merely conform to the escapist ideals fostered by mainstream Hollywood, strove to bring a personal vision to the screen and, in so doing, created lasting works of art that transcend the narrow definition of film as entertainment, pure and simple.[1]

This somewhat romanticised perspective erects a false dichotomy between the mainstream and independent sectors. Indeed, an indie film can be as conservative and generic, and designed purely to entertain, as any mainstream title. Lionsgate, for instance, mentioned in the previous chapter, has been responsible for producing and/or distributing two films based on the comic book character *The Punisher* (Hensleigh, 2004; Alexander, 2008), action movie *Crank* and its sequel *Crank: High Voltage* (Neveldine/Taylor, 2006 and 2009), *Bratz: The Movie* (McNamara, 2007) and all seven instalments of the *Saw* franchise (2004–2010) to date.

However, there is a truth at the source of the quotation: that there is more freedom to experiment and innovate away from studio pressures, whether those are generic, financial, connected to an imposed schedule, or otherwise.

Film directors of the last few decades who have worked independently – from Spike Lee to Steven Soderbergh, Jim Jarmusch to Todd Haynes – are often discussed as 'auteurs'. Although not an incorrect label to apply, this usage of the term differs from its original meaning within film criticism. The 'auteur' model of film authorship was first developed in the 1950s by a number of French critics working for the journal *Cahiers du cinéma*, including future filmmaker François Truffaut. Following World War II, a large number of Hollywood studio films that had been prevented from reaching Europe during the years of conflict started to turn up en masse. Fans and critics were therefore able to watch several films by, say, Howard Hawks, John Ford or Alfred Hitchcock in quick succession. Even though such directors were working within the Hollywood studio system, with its production line mentality, it was clear to some critical observers that Hawks et al were able to put their own stamp on the movies they were hired to helm. Predominantly, this 'stamp' was evident in visual style, from distinctive uses of mise-en-scène to characteristic camerawork. The sign of the true auteur, then, was the ability to express a creative personality consistently across several movies, even while working within the confines of the studio system.

The term 'auteur' has subsequently become used in a more generalised and widespread fashion, to refer to directors who are able to exert control over their output (whether for the studios or working independently), particularly those who deploy a consistent set of stylistic devices and repeatedly explore the same thematic tropes. Thus, Quentin Tarantino is seen as an auteur for his repeated experiments with narrative structure, quotations from cinema's history of trash and genre fictions, snappy and vulgar dialogue, play with generic form (gangster film, blaxploitation, and so on), idiosyncratic soundtracks and dazzling moments of visual spectacle. Indeed, so prominent is the understanding of Tarantino's work as the product of an auteur that critical analyses of his career will often also incorporate commentary on the films based on his screenplays (such as Tony Scott's *True Romance*, 1993) and the occasional episodes of long-running television series (*ER*, *CSI: Crime Scene Investigation*) that he has directed.

This is not to say, however, that the auteurist model of film author-ship has gone unchallenged. As early as 1962, Ian Cameron argued in the journal *Movie* that the *Cahiers du cinéma* paradigm of the auteur director managing to make their mark on mainstream films was flawed:

Hollywood films are not so much custom-built as manufactured. The responsibility for them is shared, and the final quality is no more the fault of the director than of such parties as the producer, the set designer, the cameraman, or the hairdresser. Only by a happy accident can anything good escape from this industrial complex.[2]

Even *Far from Heaven* producer Christine Vachon is critical of the auteurist paradigm, whilst recognising its significance to the market:

People are obsessed with auteurs, they want one person to be responsible for the whole film. Of course, they know that's not true – it's not the way film-making works; there are too many people involved in the making of the film. [However] I promote auteurism all the time because it's a great way to sell a movie. People don't want to hear from directors, 'I made this movie with the help of so and so, and so and so.' They want to be able to look at one person – usually a man – and say, 'Oh, that's the boy genius who made this movie!' That's what people love.[3]

The auteurist model of authorship, then, contributes to the perpetuation of the romantic ideal of the individual creative genius that remains widespread in many Western countries. It also serves the marketing and advertising for movies well, in enabling the framing of a particular title as the product of an 'artist' with an established track record.

This chapter explores the notion of authorship in relation to *Far from Heaven*. It begins by adopting an auteurist perspective; the first section is devoted to identifying the manifold ways in which the movie can be understood as 'a Todd Haynes film'. However, as an argument can be made that Haynes's work has regularly questioned the notion of film authorship, subsequent sections expand this framework and offer alternative perspectives on *Far from Heaven*. In its meticulous recreation of the Sirkian style, should Haynes's film be understood as a work of simulation? The second section unpacks the concept of simulation, and explores the impact it can have on a film director's signature. Of course, *Far from Heaven* is not merely a Sirk simulation; it is also densely inter-textual. Section three therefore looks at the notion of pastiche and asks: when a film is largely constructed from quotations, in what way is it the 'work' of its creator? Further, is pastiche always merely empty appropriation, a stylistic game, or can it serve more valuable ends? The uses of pastiche by different types of cinema are explored, as are different evaluative approaches to pastiche as a concept.

Far from Heaven as 'a Todd Haynes film'

In the opening credits of *Far from Heaven*, after the names of the production companies appear, audiences are informed they are watching 'a film by Todd Haynes'. The same words appeared on the poster for the movie, which also served as the cover of the rental and sell-through DVD (see Figure 3). This brands *Far from Heaven* as the work of a particular individual, and enables its categorisation with Haynes's other films. However, in what ways is *Far from Heaven* 'a film by Todd Haynes'? That is, what does it have in common with the rest of his œuvre? For viewers who had only previously seen *Velvet Goldmine*, for instance, Haynes's hyperbolic queer glam rock fantasia, it might be difficult to comprehend the formally rigorous generic homage of *Far from Heaven* as a product of the same director.

Figure 3 The poster used to advertise and promote *Far from Heaven* (© Focus Features/Vulcan Productions)

One aspect that connects together Haynes's films to date is that they have all been 'period dramas', even if the historical eras being referenced are not especially distant; *Safe*, for example, made in the mid-1990s, is set in the late 1980s. Of course, as is evident with *Far from Heaven*, the primary references being drawn on by Haynes in the recreation of a specific time may be from the movies and television, rather than the 'reality' of the period. *Far from Heaven* is set in 1957 to 1958; the inclusion of a televised speech by Eisenhower clearly dates the timeframe within which the film's narrative unfolds. However, the film's visual style, as identified in the previous chapter, is taken largely from Sirkian melodramas of the mid- to late 1950s. Similarly, the 'Horror' thread in *Poison* borrows its style from infection-themed horror films of the 1950s, rather than attempting to depict that decade authentically. And although the scenes featuring Cate Blanchett in *I'm Not There* faithfully recreate documentary footage of Bob Dylan in interview and concert, other narrative threads are more deliberately fictional – such as that starring Richard Gere as Billy the Kid, set in a version of the Old West, which references Dylan's role in *Pat Garrett and Billy the Kid* (Peckinpah, 1973). Haynes's 'historical fictions', then, question the boundaries between real, mediated and fictional representations of different time periods, and the implications of these collapsing into each other in cultural memory.

Critical discussions of Haynes's films often articulate connections between specific titles. Indeed, James Morrison suggests that 'later films often seem to "answer" earlier ones, to extend or play out the uncompleted intellectual projects of earlier work.'[4] Based on their protagonists, Haynes's œuvre has been divided by several critics into his 'male' films (*Assassins*, *Poison*, *Velvet Goldmine*, *I'm Not There*) and his 'female' films (*Superstar*, *Safe*, *Far from Heaven*), which he has alternated between during his career. Certainly, all three 'female' films are linked in their narrative focus on a suffering woman who is oppressed by social and cultural pressures: ideal body image, how to be a perfect mother and housewife, and so on. Haynes himself, in a book of three of his screenplays, connects the 'female' movies together:

These are my women's films – two features and an oblong short – that belong to one another as much as they do to me. In a way they are sisters, and if there exists between them a sisterhood of sorts, aligning them as stories about women or even experiments in form, the imprint of feminism would clearly be at its core [. . .] In all three of these films, each of which inflicts upon its heroine a dangerous upheaval, identification itself is put in peril. In each case there is something that stands between the central character and ourselves.[5]

Here, Haynes not only acknowledges the influence of feminism on his own thinking (to which I return below), but also identifies the fact that a key concern in his filmmaking practice has been to interrogate the mechanics of audience identification with characters. In *Superstar* this involves using dolls as actors, whereas in *Far from Heaven* the emulation of the artificial Sirkian look and the adoption of an outmoded performance style both serve as initial barriers between characters and contemporary viewers. Haynes's interest in this subject – how audiences identify with characters, despite hurdles – is also explored in some of his 'male' films; the fragmented approach to Bob Dylan's character in *I'm Not There*, for instance, is an experiment not dissimilar to that attempted by Todd Solondz in *Palindromes* (2004), in which the protagonist Aviva is played by ten actors of different ages, races and genders.

Haynes studied Art and Semiotics at Brown University, and subsequently attained an MFA from Bard College. He was heavily influenced by a combination of women's studies and film theory at Brown, and has carried his theoretical knowledge with him throughout his career, often discussing aspects of his practice in relation to particular concepts and ideas, as well as examples from his extensive knowledge of the history of cinema. (During his director's commentary on the *Far from Heaven* DVD, for instance, Haynes sometimes reads out quotes from key Film Studies texts on melodrama, including Fassbinder's writings on Douglas Sirk and Jon Halliday's book-length interview with Sirk.) For some critics, this is a concern, as it can reduce Haynes's films to little more than intellectual experimentation, the practical exploration of specific theories. Keith Uhlich, for instance, in an appreciative article on Haynes, nevertheless concedes that the director's work is 'a very literary experience, a cinema where you feel (or read) through the idea, as opposed to the more commonplace occurrence where viewer passivity is the order of the day'.[6] As Mary Ann Doane writes,

Critical reviews of Haynes's work often evince a nervous anxiety about what they refer to as the Brown-educated filmmaker's status as an intellectual. This is undoubtedly at least partially due to a pervasive anti-intellectualism in American public discourse, but it is also connected to the recalcitrance of the binary opposition between intellect and emotion. Even in relation to highly accessible films such as *Safe* and *Far from Heaven*, the charge that the films are cold, cynical, or overwrought is present.[7]

Doane and others have countered such charges and argued that, despite Haynes's professed interest in placing formal barriers in the way of audience identification with his characters, films such as *Superstar* and *Far from Heaven* have the ability to reduce their viewers to tears. The specific mechanics of this process will be explored in more detail in Chapter 3.

One of the elements of his education at Brown that seems to have had a significant impact on Haynes's thinking, and on his films, is a particular approach to understanding gender and identity. Theories of postmodernism/postmodernity were being developed and popularised during the 1980s; Fredric Jameson's article, 'Postmodernism, or the Cultural Logic of Late Capitalism', first appeared in the journal *New Left Review* in 1984, the same year that the English translation of Jean-François Lyotard's *The Postmodern Condition* was published. These texts (and others) identified significant challenges to modernist 'metanarratives' (such as the notion of progress through science) and particular bodies of thought (such as Marxism), and associated attempts to inaugurate a more pluralistic, relativistic and anti-hierarchical attitude and politics. At around the same time, the body of ideas and approaches known collectively as post-structuralism began to attain significant critical currency. Post-structuralism has its roots in writings of the 1960s by critics such as Umberto Eco (*Opera aperta*, 1962) and Roland Barthes (originally a structuralist, whose post-structuralist phase arguably begins with his 1968 essay 'The Death of the Author').[8] The field developed in the 1970s through the work of such figures as Gilles Deleuze and Félix Guattari (*Capitalisme et schizophrénie 1: L'Anti-Œdipe* [1972]) and Michel Foucault (*Surveiller et punir* [1975]; *Histoire de la sexualité, Vol 1: La Volonté de savoir* [1976]).[9] Post-structuralism, as the name implies, countered the tenets of structuralism, proposing (for instance) that the 'self' is a fictional construct, and that the meaning an author gives to a text is of secondary importance to that perceived by the reader. These two streams of thought (postmodernism and post-structuralism) were taken up, taught and debated in universities during the 1980s (and subsequently), in subject areas from English to Philosophy, from Film Studies to Women's Studies. For many minorities, the alleged end of the era of modernity suggested the potential arrival of a new period of social and political equivalence for all. An understanding of identity as largely culturally constructed – and therefore malleable and open to contestation – began to attain substantial currency. In the late 1980s and early 1990s, post-structuralist ideas were influential in the genesis of the body of critical writing known as queer theory – a topic explored in detail in Chapter 4.

Throughout his career, Haynes has used his films to interrogate and challenge the limitations of specific identity categories and social roles: the bluntness of labels, the oppressive nature of certain culturally constructed positions, the role of the media in fixing an identity. This is especially clear in *Poison*'s three narrative strands. In 'Homo', criminal John Broom (Scott Renderer) has a relationship with a fellow male prisoner; in 'Horror', a scientist accidentally drinks an isolated sex serum, physically mutates and deteriorates, and goes on the run; in 'Hero', a young boy commits patricide and disappears. The behaviour of all three protagonists falls outside of the boundaries of 'normal' behaviour. At various points in the three narrative strands, representatives of 'normal' society attempt to explain, label or categorise their behaviour, but those terms and explanations are clearly inadequate and partial, at worst misguided and pejorative. In *Safe*, Carol White is an upper-middle-class suburban 'homemaker', but her lack of fit with the role is made steadily apparent; she is unable to relate to her step-son, recoils from her husband's embrace and is traumatised by the delivery of a sofa that is the wrong colour. She starts to become ill, wheezing at a child's birthday party, collapsing at the dry cleaner's store. Doctors fail to diagnose her symptoms; Carol comes to believe she has 'environmental illness'. But even after she retreats to a desert commune, her health fails to improve, and she ends the film isolated, gaunt and scarred. *Far from Heaven* also offers its own critique of identity categories: Frank cannot live up to the standards of the 1950s company-and-family-man because he is hiding his homosexuality; Cathy falls for a black man, and painfully discovers the impermeability of the social boundaries between races.

In addition to the impact on Haynes's films of the education he received at Brown, another formative influence was working with Gran Fury. Haynes was, in fact, one of the founders of Gran Fury, the activist art organisation based in New York and affiliated to ACT-UP (AIDS Coalition To Unleash Power). Gran Fury designed and distributed posters and flyers, using the rhetoric and methods of advertising in order to raise public awareness of the shoddy responses by government, the healthcare system and big business to the AIDS crisis. The activist group challenged the attribution of blame used to marginalise people with HIV/AIDS prevalent at the time (one poster read 'All People With AIDS Are Innocent'), and promoted safer sex practices ('Men: Use Condoms or Beat It,' said one flier). They also directly targeted figures with power and influence who were ignoring the spread of HIV/AIDS; fake banknotes distributed on Wall Street had 'Fuck your profiteering: People are dying while you play business' printed on their flipside. Haynes's involvement with the angry direct action politics of Gran Fury and ACT-UP can be seen in his filmmaking in two main topics: a recurrent bringing to light of the oppressive circumstances within which many minorities are trapped; and a repeated return to AIDS as subject matter, however obliquely treated.

José Arroyo, in an essay on New Queer Cinema, has argued that HIV/AIDS operated as the political unconscious of the short-lived film movement, and was a significant factor binding the work of its directors together.[10] In some titles, such as Gregg Araki's *The Living End* (1992), HIV and AIDS were handled directly; in others, including *My Own Private Idaho* (Van Sant, 1991), allegorical or metaphorical treatment displaced the disease on to other illnesses or conditions. Regarding Haynes's œuvre, Karen Carpenter's wasting sickness in *Superstar*, Dr Graves's physical deterioration in *Poison* and Carol's 'environmental illness' in *Safe* can all be read as commentaries on HIV/AIDS. Indeed, Haynes stated in an interview in 1996 that all of his films to date had been about illness, because of AIDS.[11] In contrast, the disease is not a manifestly evident context in relation to his subsequent films, *Velvet Goldmine*, *Far from Heaven* and *I'm Not There*. However, in Chapter 4 I will explore the possibility that *Far from Heaven*'s mournful tone and its pervasive register of melancholia can be understood as influenced by queer political responses to HIV/AIDS.

Smaller elements connect *Far from Heaven* to other films by Haynes. In relation to casting, Barbara Garrick (playing Cathy's friend Doreen) appeared as Stevie's mother in *Dottie Gets Spanked*. Lines of dialogue connect Karen Carpenter (*Superstar*), Carol White (*Safe*) and Cathy. All three cover over trauma and hurt by faking a veneer of stable health and well-being. Karen, on the phone to her doctor, tells him she is 'doing great – feel super! Better than ever!' just moments before she overdoses on emetics; Carol, speaking to her mother on the phone, tells her 'All right, that's fine, he's fine, they're fine,' but is then seriously stressed when she sees the new couch that has been delivered; Cathy, accidentally smacked in the forehead by Frank, quickly says 'It's all right, I'm all right.' The bruise on Cathy's forehead is mirrored by that on Carol's at the end of *Safe*. Both Carol and Cathy try to find isolated spaces, away from the gaze of others, in order to cry – Carol in her cabin at the commune, Cathy in her garden – but both are disturbed in their weeping by the arrival of other people. Conventional medicine is ineffectual in both *Safe* and *Far from Heaven*. Carol's rejections of her husband's sexual advances in *Safe* are echoed in Frank's inability to have sex with Cathy. Bullying children hurl prejudicial epithets in *Poison*, *Dottie Gets Spanked* and *Far from Heaven*. Although these aspects are all relatively minor, they reveal the subtle ways in which a director may replay or rework touches of their previous output.

One final topic that can be seen to tie together Haynes's films – and arguably the most significant for this chapter's discussions – is his broader concern with the notion of authorship and originality. As James Morrison writes,

Todd Haynes has built an original style out of simulation – intricately mannered yet emotionally immediate – and it is now one of the most suggestive styles in American movies. Haynes' work is indispensable in considering some of the most pressing questions of contemporary culture . . . [For instance,] at a time when even the concept of authenticity is under siege, can the artist, especially if the artist is a filmmaker, hope to achieve or work from any viable position of originality, or is originality itself simply another myth of the modernist imagination that postmodern art itself has done so much in recent decades to demystify?[12]

In his previous films, Haynes had consciously 'borrowed' elements from particular genres, or the films of specific directors, in order to explore the impact of such practices. *Safe* is indebted to Antonioni, Fassbinder, Kubrick and Sirk; components of *Citizen Kane* (Welles, 1941) crop up in *Velvet Goldmine*; and so on. However, the thorough and consistent adoption of the Sirkian style in *Far from Heaven* pushes this interrogation of originality and authorship further than any of Haynes's other films, inviting viewers to ask: what does it mean to borrow so wholeheartedly from another director's work?

Simulation and De-authorisation

Reviews and critical discussions of *Far from Heaven* routinely refer to the film as a simulation or a pastiche of the films of Douglas Sirk.

Sometimes these terms and others have been used negatively, to criticise the movie and imply redundancy or a lack of originality. ('The
problem with *Far from Heaven* isn't that it's an imitation of life but
that it's an imitation of *Imitation of Life*,' wrote Stephen Hunter in *The
Washington Post*.[13]) As just noted, the sustained form of simulation on
display in *Far from Heaven* is of a different order to, and extends far
beyond the intertextual borrowings of, Haynes's earlier films. Here,
rather than an allusion or reference, one particular style – incorporating
script, décor, camera movement, lighting, costume, soundtrack and
performance codes – is adopted for the entire running time of the
film. In this section of this chapter, I want to consider *Far from Heaven*'s
extreme degree of simulation, and its influence on the film's authorship. Specifically, I will argue that it substantially 'de-authorises' *Far
from Heaven*, in a manner that complicates understandings of the movie
as 'a Todd Haynes film'.

The extensive simulation and recreation of another director's style
adopted in *Far from Heaven* is rather rare in cinema. However, valuable comparisons can be made between Haynes's film and others.
Gus Van Sant's 1998 remake of Alfred Hitchcock's *Psycho* (which also
starred Julianne Moore) is almost a shot-for-shot reconstruction of the
original, with the main differences between the two versions being a
change of setting to the late 1990s, the choice of colour stock, the cast
and some minor updatings to the script. Guy Maddin's film *Careful*
(1992), in contrast, is indebted to the Bergfilme, the genre of silent
mountain adventure movies produced in Germany in the 1920s – in
particular, Arnold Frank's *The Holy Mountain* (1926). *Careful*, like *Far from
Heaven*, meticulously attempts to recreate the aesthetic of the period:
in Maddin's case, with hand-tinted frames, intertitles and scratched/
degraded imagery. All three of these films can be seen as concerted
attempts by their directors to challenge critical understandings of
authorship, especially their own careers as 'auteurs'. The movies ask: if a
director rigorously mimics works of cinema history, then to what extent
is the resultant film their own?

For James Morrison, *Far from Heaven* marks the peak of what he calls
'Haynes' project of achieving a state of pure simulation'.[14] He refers to
the writings of French philosopher Jean Baudrillard who, in *Simulacra
and Simulations* (1981) and other texts, argues pessimistically that a defining characteristic of the postmodern era is a predominance of simulations which mimic reality and then begin to take its place. Baudrillard

observes a historical shift to a period in which there is a lack of distinction between objects and representations, one dominated by simulacra which absorb the real within themselves, leaving us with a 'hyperreality', a system of signs which only make sense in relation to each other. He expresses particular concern about films which effectively recreate earlier historical periods, including *Chinatown* (Polanski, 1974), *Barry Lyndon* (Kubrick, 1975) and *1900* (Bertolucci, 1976):

Take *The Last Picture Show* [Bogdanovich, 1971]: like me, you would have had to be sufficiently distracted to have thought it to be an original production from the 1950s: a very good film about the customs in and the atmosphere of the American small town. Just a slight suspicion: it was a little too good, more in tune, better than the others, without the psychological, moral, and sentimental blotches of the films of that era. Stupefaction when one discovers that it is a 1970s film, perfect retro, purged, pure, the hyperrealist restitution of 1950s cinema [. . .] A whole generation of films is emerging that will be to those one knew what the android is to man: marvellous artefacts, without weakness, pleasing simulacra that lack only the imaginary, and the hallucination inherent to cinema. Most of what we see today (the best) is already of this order [. . .] All the toxic radiation has been filtered, all the ingredients are there, in precise doses, not a single error.[15]

Baudrillard is not the only writer to have made this argument about the movies – Fredric Jameson also critiques what he calls 'la mode retro' in cinema[16] – but he certainly pursues it most tenaciously. And it is indeed possible to see *Far from Heaven* through Baudrillard's lens, as 'perfect retro', a simulation of Sirk that improves on the original with contemporary production values (a wider screen format, higher-grade film stock, better sound quality). Baudrillard's pessimism, however, seems to be rooted both in his own inability to differentiate the simulation from the original, and in his diagnosis that the source has been replaced by the imitator. Yet, in the case of *Far from Heaven*, alternative arguments could be made: that audiences are able to tell the difference clearly between Todd Haynes's film and Douglas Sirk's output (the contemporary cast is a bit of a giveaway), which only enhances their viewing pleasure; and that Haynes's movie might operate as a spur to some viewers to rediscover the original melodramas being simulated.

Resisting the negative critique inherent in Baudrillard's arguments, Morrison identifies their use value when considering the ways in which Haynes confronts the subject of originality:

As Jean Baudrillard argues most notably, simulation is central to the postmodern sensibility because it follows from, and marks, the passing of origin and originality. Once everything has already been done, once subjects are dead and condemned to nothing but the re-enactment of given scenarios, once feelings have all already been played out, what is left to postmodern culture is the aesthetic of simulation, and though all of Haynes' work is dependent on that aesthetic, *Far from Heaven* is the fullest realisation of it. In Haynes, as in Baudrillard, the aesthetic of simulation denies the idea of essence: To imitate a prior text is to apprehend its essence and honour a preceding point of origin, but to simulate it is to imply that its materials are transportable, without defining reference to their initial contexts.[17]

For Morrison, then, Haynes's simulation of Sirk is a tactic of destabilisation, intended to undermine the notion of a stable 'essence'. Sirk becomes 'Sirk', a system of aesthetic devices and narrative tropes that can be easily emulated and reproduced in the present day. 'Authorship' is transformed into a loose concept that links a particular stylistic/ formal/thematic 'system' to a named person – but which can easily be dis-articulated from them. Haynes can 'do' or 'perform' 'Sirk'; and in *Far from Heaven*, he performs 'Sirk' almost wholesale, all but disappearing behind the impersonation. This 'loss' of Haynes may explain why some fans of his work (myself included) were initially disappointed with *Far from Heaven*: the Sirk mask was seamlessly worn.

It is not surprising that Haynes and Van Sant have attempted such experiments at 'de-authorisation'; film authorship has been a fundamental concern for many lesbian/gay/queer directors, historians and theorists. (Maddin is a rogue example, though he has noted, rather queerly, that 'I've been called the gayest straight filmmaker and the straightest gay filmmaker.'[18]) Historically and politically, in a culture dominated by the silences of oppression and the closet, it has been vital for lesbian and gay filmmakers to be able to identify themselves as the authors of their work. This is especially true for those films which have been produced 'independently' and which proclaim their sexual orientation loudly and lucidly. As Richard Dyer notes,

The idea of authority implied in that of authorship, the feeling that it is a way of claiming legitimacy and power for a text's meanings and affects, is indeed what is at issue in overtly lesbian/gay texts. They are about claiming the right to speak as lesbian/gay, claiming a special authority for their image of lesbianism/gayness because it is produced by people who are themselves lesbian/gay.[19]

However, both Haynes and Van Sant began their filmmaking careers after postmodern/post-structuralist challenges to the status of the author – in Barthes's essay 'Death of the Author', for instance, and Foucault's 'What is an Author?' – had attained significant status and influence.[20] These bodies of theory also undermined the notion of identities as stable entities, emphasising instead understandings of 'the self' as culturally constructed. Indeed, many queer film directors have, over the last twenty years or so, needed to square a desire to contribute to a history of queer representation with their recognition that 'authorship' is a contested concept, and that their own sexual orientation may be culturally produced, rather than innate. Richard Dyer proposes one way out of this quandary. Noting that the author is 'an authority concept, anti-democratic in its triumphant individualism, a support for existing social divisions, hostile to public discourses, and resistant to the creativity of the reader'[21] but desiring to somehow maintain a politically effective queer identity, he puts forward a model

of multiple authorship (with varying degrees of hierarchy and control) in specific determining economic and technological circumstances, all those involved always working with (within and against) particular codes and conventions of film and with (within and against) particular, social ways of being lesbian and gay [. . .] In this perspective both authorship and being lesbian/gay become a kind of performance, something we all do but only with the terms, the discourses, available to us, and whose relationship to any imputed self doing the performing cannot be taken as read [. . .] This model of authorship as performance hangs onto the notion of the author as a real, material person, but in . . . a 'decentred' way.[22]

The gay/lesbian/queer director, then, can retain their sexual orientation and their ability to author their work, but this entails the recognition that both of these fragile, complicated concepts are strategically harnessed and deployed for political ends. Both *Psycho* and *Far from Heaven* can be seen as extreme engagements with this complex nexus of concerns. Haynes mimics Sirk; Van Sant impersonates Hitchcock. Haynes and Van Sant had already established 'auteur' careers that included queerness as a constituent component of their 'stamp'. In their simulation of Hitchcock and Sirk, however, *Psycho* and *Far from Heaven* seemed like their respective directors' least queer films. (This has not prevented theorists from interpreting these films queerly, of course, as Janet Staiger has done with Van Sant's film,[23] and as I do with *Far from Heaven* in Chapter 4 of this book.) 'Haynes' and 'Van Sant', as established and recognisable auteurist styles, seemed to be tempered or tamed by 'Sirk' and 'Hitchcock', the present-day directors' signatures largely submerged beneath those of their precedents. Impersonating a canonical director is an ambitious enterprise, and Van Sant arguably took the greater risk. While *Far from Heaven* was mainly well received by critics, Van Sant's 'experiment' was lambasted by a significant number of writers. (Jonathan Rosenbaum, for instance, called the film 'a piece of dead meat'.[24]) Setting aside the quality of Van Sant's *Psycho*, these responses seem to reveal the broader cultural standing of Hitchcock in comparison with Sirk.

The tension between mainstream and independent cinema is also in operation in the 'de-authorisation' of these queer directors suggested by *Psycho* and *Far from Heaven*. There is a lengthy history of lesbian/gay/queer independent film work made outside of the studio system in the US, expressing a non-heterosexual perspective, but the number of mainstream directors known to be queer is negligible. Several queer film historians have successfully examined the careers of figures such as Dorothy Arzner and George Cukor for signs that their sexual 'otherness' impacted on their films.[25] Similar arguments could be made with other figures, such as Roland Emmerich, director of *Godzilla* (1998), *The Day After Tomorrow* (2004) and *2012* (2010). However, discerning the 'queerness' hidden in the work of these mainstream directors often feels like extremely exhausting archaeology for tiny bits of sparkly shrapnel, as though the limitations and pressures of the studio system largely prevent any such expressions from taking shape. *Psycho* and *Far from Heaven* were both made with studio assistance, thus serving as rare instances of queer, experimental directors being given Hollywood funding. In their 'de-authorisation' of these two films, then, Van Sant and Haynes may be commenting on the restrictions that queer directors have to operate within should they choose to make mainstream movies. If you are queer and you want to work for the studios, these two films seem to say, you will have to emulate one of the established forms and styles, and largely disavow your own identity.

Pastiche

Although *Far from Heaven* simulates the style associated with a particular director, unlike Van Sant's *Psycho*, it does not re-present one specific film. Rather, its fabric (narrative, characters, lines of dialogue, incidental moments of framing) is in significant part assembled from a broad array of other texts – an array that includes films by Sirk, Ophüls, Preminger, Fassbinder and others. Thus, although 'simulation' is a crucial concept for exploring *Far from Heaven*'s form and authorship, it is also necessary to frame Haynes's film in relation to pastiche – another term that regularly appears throughout critical explorations and evaluations of the movie. In this section, I want to explore the extent of the pastiche in *Far from Heaven*, the relationship between independent cinema and pastiche, and, drawing on particular theoretical understandings of the concept, propose that *Far from Heaven*'s extensive allusions to and borrowings from cinema history are a political tactic through which Todd Haynes challenges traditional notions of film authorship. In Chapters 3 and 4, I will further explore the topic of pastiche, identifying the ways in which *Far from Heaven*'s referencing of other films has a significant impact on its meaning, relationship to cinema history, and textual politics.

Of course, it is important to specify that *Far from Heaven* is not simply constituted from elements of other films, sutured together to produce an experimental whole. A number of avant-garde directors have produced work of this sort, however, and it is instructive to contrast such films with *Far from Heaven*. Bruce Conner's short film *A Movie* (1958) and Bill Morrison's *Decasia* (2002), for instance, are both assembled solely from found fragments of stock. As an extreme example, Anne McGuire's *Strain Andromeda The* (1992) takes Robert Wise's science fiction film *The Andromeda Strain* (1971) and re-edits it shot by shot, so that the entire film happens in reverse. Ken Jacobs's *Star Spangled to Death* (2004), more than six hours in length, edits together appropriated footage from movie and television history, alongside some original filmed material. *Far from Heaven* is also distinct from studio comedy *Dead Men Don't Wear Plaid* (Carl Reiner, 1982), which incorporates extracts from classic Hollywood movies into its content – Steve Martin seeming to have a phone conversation with Barbara Stanwyck, for instance, even though her moments are taken from *Sorry, Wrong Number* (Litvak, 1948). (The only borrowed film clip in *Far from Heaven* is from *The Three Faces of Eve* (Johnson, 1957), but this is a diegetic element, watched by one of the film's characters.) Rather, *Far from Heaven*'s form of assemblage is more subtle, the echoes and allusions incorporated into moments and scenes of newly filmed material. Indeed, perverse though the analogy may seem, *Far from Heaven*'s pastiche is not unlike that of Tarantino's

Figure 4 The opening moments of *All That Heaven Allows* . . . (© Universal Studios)

Pulp Fiction (1994); although the 'originality' of the completed project allows it to be enjoyed 'straight' by a wide audience, the cinephile can be rewarded for spotting the multiple references to examples of film history.

Of course, the films of Douglas Sirk are a major reference point in *Far from Heaven*, especially *All That Heaven Allows*. Even the titles of the movies are similar, connecting heaven and a sense of space – though Haynes's title hints at his film's downbeat conclusion, where Sirk's implies his happy ending (however artificially grafted on, and irrespective of his stated opinion that 'heaven is stingy'[26]). At the level of narrative, the connection between these two films is most notable in the focus on a romance between a middle-class woman and her gardener – Cary (Jane Wyman) and Ron (Rock Hudson), Cathy and Raymond – and the social approbation and rejection subsequently experienced by the women. However, there are other more subtle elements. Haynes's opening camera movement, from the branches of a tree down to the streets of Hartford, is clearly indebted to the opening moments of *All That Heaven Allows*; the station wagon that Cathy drives is even the same colour as that of Cary's friend Sara (see Figures 4 and 5). Cathy and Raymond discuss the spiritual possibilities of abstract art, concentrating on a painting by Miró; Cary and Ron discuss literature, specifically Walden's *Thoreau*. Ron and Raymond are even sometimes clothed in similar ways, with both favouring flannel.

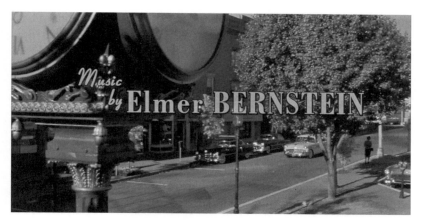

Figure 5 . . . and of *Far from Heaven* (© Focus Features/Vulcan Productions)

However, elements of other Sirk films also resonate through the texture of *Far from Heaven*. The relationship between Cathy and her housekeeper, Sybil, resembles that between Lora Meredith (Lana Turner) and Annie Johnson (Juanita Moore) in *Imitation of Life* (1959), especially in similar conversations between them concerning how the maid can find the time to do community work in addition to her paid labour. Further, as Jonathan Rosenbaum comments,

A neurotic character going ballistic when he can't summon up an erection inevitably becomes a gloss on Robert Stack's impotent millionaire in *Written on the Wind* [1956]; a beneficent-looking shrink in a bow tie and vest recalls a key spiritual guru in *Magnificent Obsession* [1954].

Dan Sallitt also suggests a connection to *There's Always Tomorrow* (1956), in the way both films handle 'the fusion of corporate and family life'.[27] And, as discussed in the previous chapter, the homosexuality plotline in *Far from Heaven* can be seen as an acknowledgement by Haynes of the closeted sexuality of Rock Hudson, who played romantic lead for Sirk in a number of films.

Aside from Sirk, other directors are referenced in *Far from Heaven*. A key figure here is Max Ophüls. Haynes has conceded that he borrowed from *The Reckless Moment* (1949): Cathy weeping on her bed near the conclusion of Haynes's film is framed identically to a similar moment when Lucia Harper (Joan Bennett) cries in the movie by Ophüls; further, the

Figure 6 The television set is delivered in *All That Heaven Allows* (© Universal Studios)

Whitakers' maid Sybil (Viola Davis) is named after the Harpers' help.[28] The sons in the two films are both called David, and are regularly ordered to behave properly by their mothers: 'David, put your shirt on' in Ophüls, 'David, put your bike away and help Sybil with the groceries' in Haynes, for instance.[29] *Far from Heaven*, *The Reckless Moment* and Sirk's *All That Heaven Allows* all feature scenes set at Christmas, in which the festive decorations and attempts at upbeat celebrations are ironically played against and undermined by viewer knowledge of thinly concealed emotional turmoil. Cary's children buy her a television to prevent her from feeling lonely and as a substitute for her relationship with Ron (see Figure 6); Lucia weeps on the phone to her husband discussing the Christmas tree, unable to tell him about the blackmail plot she has managed to extricate herself from (see Figure 7); Cathy's Christmas gift to Frank is a holiday to Miami, where he abandons her poolside in order to have sex with a blond youth. In addition to *The Reckless Moment*, critics have suggested associations between *Far from Heaven* and other films by Ophüls. Although Haynes has stated that his film's concluding moments, in which Cathy waves goodbye to Raymond, recall a similar scene from Hitchcock's *Marnie* (1964),[30] Dana Luciano draws a comparison with Ophüls's *Letter from an Unknown Woman* (1948). She goes further: highlighting the circularity of *Far from Heaven*'s plot, with Cathy beginning and ending the film 'driving the family station wagon through the town square', Luciano argues that

Figure 7 Lucia Harper crying in *The Reckless Moment* (© Columbia Pictures Corp.)

This recourse to the gesture of repetitive return recalls Max Ophüls's celebrated 'women's films' of the late 1940s, *Letter from an Unknown Woman* (1948) and *The Reckless Moment* (1949), which leave their protagonists (both mothers with illicit romantic attachments) pointedly going nowhere – either dead or 'imprisoned' within domesticity.[31]

Although this broader structural similarity certainly does connect *Far from Heaven* with more than one of Ophüls's films, the circular narrative form is also typical of many other melodramas. (The constituent components of melodrama as a genre will be discussed in detail in Chapter 3.)

In addition to Ophüls, a further director whose work is alluded to by *Far from Heaven* is Otto Preminger. Haynes has stated that the visit Frank pays to a gay bar near the beginning of his film is a reference to a similar scene in Preminger's *Advise and Consent* (1962).[32] Dan Sallitt identifies additional connections:

Other hints of Preminger are probably due only to a certain temperamental affinity between the two directors. But one notes in passing a visual and dynamic similarity between Dennis Haysbert's farewell to Julianne Moore and the equivalent scene with Dana Andrews and Joan Crawford in Preminger's *Daisy Kenyon* [1947]. And the spasmodic blocking of the scene in which Moore discovers Quaid in flagrante delicto in his office evokes the Preminger of *Bunny Lake is Missing* [1965] or *Hurry Sundown* [1967] more than it does Sirk's elegant stasis.[33]

The German director Rainer Werner Fassbinder is also a key influence on *Far from Heaven*. Fassbinder was a fan of Sirk's melodramas, and wrote appreciatively of their power and importance. His 1974 film *Fear Eats the Soul* (*Angst essen Seele auf*) is a loose remake of Sirk's *All That Heaven Allows*, following the relationship between Emmi (Brigitte Mira), an elderly white German cleaning woman, and Ali (El Hedi ben Salem), a much younger black Moroccan immigrant. The racial difference between these characters is mirrored in that between Cathy and Raymond. Other moments in Haynes's film seem to be indebted to Fassbinder's version of Sirk. Cathy and Raymond's dance in the black bar, Ernie's, is reminiscent in tempo and lighting of a similar moment between Emmi and Ali at the Asphalt Bar. The couples in both films receive cold receptions in restaurants and cafés: Emmi and Ali are treated disdainfully by a waiter when they eat at Osteria Italiana; when Cathy meets Raymond at a drugstore, the soda jerk asks 'Is there something I can do for you folks?' with a frown, prompting them to leave. Individual lines of dialogue also recur: Emmi says to Ali 'You are so beautiful,' which Cathy also says to Raymond as they stand outside the cinema.[34]

As if these borrowings from Sirk, Ophüls, Preminger and Fassbinder were not enough, critics have identified further references in *Far from Heaven*. When the characters in Haynes's film visit the cinema or meet outside it, particular films are playing in double bills: *The Three Faces of Eve* and *Miracle in the Rain* (Maté, 1956); *Hilda Crane* (Dunne, 1956) and *The Bold and the Brave* (Foster, 1956). As Lynne Joyrich has argued, these are 'film pairings that mark the conflicted world in which the characters live, and texts that mark the conflicted nature of the characters' own hopes for pairing.'[35] Frank, for instance, chooses to see *The Three Faces of Eve*, the narrative of which follows the psychiatric treatment of a woman with multiple personalities; this foreshadows his own trip to the doctor for advice and assistance with his hidden identity as a homosexual. Other connections made by critics are more tenuous. Geoffrey O'Brien, for instance, says of Quaid's character that 'his anguish and shame call to mind Grant Williams as *The Incredible Shrinking Man* (1957) angrily rejecting his wife when she attempts to comfort him for his mysterious loss of masculine pride.'[36]

The lengthy list of references just outlined highlights the extent of *Far from Heaven*'s intertextual pastiche, and of Todd Haynes's knowledge of cinema history. It demonstrates, as Haynes's other films also do, that the director approaches film as a medium with an extensive archive that can be plundered and appropriated. For knowledgeable audiences, spotting the references can be an enjoyable pastime, although one that arguably bears a similarity to trainspotting. For others (somewhat ironically, given the film's content), it can be enjoyed 'straight'. This division of *Far from Heaven*'s audiences into two camps has been noted by a number of reviewers and theorists, including J. Hoberman in *The Village Voice*:

For those familiar with the Sirkian text, Haynes . . . has done a splendid job of filmed film criticism. Without resorting to camp or parody, Haynes (like Sirk, but differently) has transformed the rhetoric of Hollywood melodrama into something provocative, rich, and strange. For those who are not Sirk-literate, *Far from Heaven* may seem even more startling – a full-bodied simulation of a genre that, historically speaking, should no longer exist.[37]

The implication in this observation is that Haynes's use of pastiche in *Far from Heaven* is generative, 'transformative', productive, and not merely empty quotation or stylistic appropriation. It is worth briefly exploring, then, the various aesthetic and political ends towards which pastiche can be marshalled by different forms of cinema.

Susan Hayward has identified particular aesthetic and stylistic devices associated with postmodern cinema, including bricolage and intertextuality. She notes that both mainstream and independent (or what she terms 'oppositional') forms of cinema can make use of these tactics. Thus, for instance, each of the films in the *Scary Movie* franchise (2000–2006) intertextually references a number of different examples of the horror genre. Even a children's film such as *Cats and Dogs: The Revenge of Kitty Galore* (Peyton, 2010) opens with a sequence that quotes *The Silence of the Lambs* (Demme, 1991) – presumably only recognisable as an allusion to the adults in the audience. Hayward suggests that mainstream and 'oppositional' cinema differ in their employment of these strategies. Whereas the latter uses them for critical and political purposes, their presence in mainstream film is always merely stylistic, empty copying or borrowing with no deeper purpose. As she puts it, 'What separates the two tendencies is that the oppositional postmodern aesthetic experiments with these concepts and innovates through subverting their codes, whereas the mainstream postmodern aesthetic merely replicates them.'[38] Of course, this argument requires a clear distinction between mainstream and 'oppositional' cinema – one that films such as *Far from Heaven*, sitting on the border between the two, in 'Indiewood', trouble and problematise. It is also difficult to sustain; the use of pastiche in the independently financed *Another Gay Movie* (Stephens, 2006), for instance, is hard to distinguish from that in studio release *Epic Movie* (Friedberg/ Seltzer, 2007). However, Hayward's argument is a valuable model for thinking through the political employment of specific formal and aesthetic strategies – and, as identified in Chapter 1, independent cinema is often associated with a political perspective in contrast to films produced by the mainstream studios.

Certainly, Haynes's use of pastiche and intertextuality has repeatedly been recognised as specifically 'subversive' and political. As John David Rhodes argues, for instance, in an essay on *Safe*,

> Haynes is both an acute reader of film history and an exquisitely careful practitioner of a kind of filmmaking that incorporates and allegorically re-reads earlier film practices [. . .] For Haynes . . . film history is not just an archive of images, but rather an arsenal of aesthetic and epistemological strategies [. . .] Haynes' allegorical appropriations of earlier moments in film history are not superficial, nor are they condescending. The allegorical transparencies that he asks us to see *Safe* through, or to see through *Safe*, suggest the way in which these earlier practices that he is reworking do not fully work and are not sufficient to handle the nature of the problems he wants to address.[39]

Indeed, as will be demonstrated in Chapters 3 and 4, Haynes's extensive references to the history of melodrama in *Far from Heaven* not only engage with the historical distance between contemporary film practice and 1950s genre cinema, but also directly and tactically confront the various omissions of those earlier movies, their lacks and occlusions.

Beyond the differing uses to which pastiche can be put by filmmakers, the concept itself has often been perceived negatively, even scathingly. Perhaps most famously, theorist Fredric Jameson is especially critical of pastiche:

> Pastiche is, like parody, the imitation of a peculiar or unique, idiosyncratic style, the wearing of a linguistic mask, speech in a dead language. But it is a neutral practice of such mimicry, without any of parody's ulterior motives, amputated of the satiric impulse, devoid of laughter . . . Pastiche is thus blank parody, a statue with blind eyeballs.[40]

This approach, in which pastiche is compared unfavourably with parody, is also found in writings by Linda Hutcheon.[41] In contrast, Richard Dyer offers a spirited defence of pastiche, and one that is particularly valuable in relation to this chapter's concern with authorship. He recognises that, historically, pastiche

seems to have been especially congenial to social groupings or individuals within them who feel marginal to but not entirely excluded from the wider society . . . However, those circumstances and groupings may also simply make people more alert to a fact of the human condition: that we think and feel for ourselves and yet only by means of the frameworks of thought and feeling available to us.[42]

Pastiche, argues Dyer, poses a challenge to those who are invested in the notion of 'thinking and feeling autonomously out of the inner imperatives of the self', and who believe they 'are the centre and author of discourse':

If you have something invested in experiencing it like that, in occupying the originating position of knowledge and authority, then accepting that you are in the realm of the already said may be a source of anguish, but for others – in given circumstances, in given groupings – it is no more than what life is like and one had better get used to it. Pastiche articulates this sense of living permanently, ruefully but without distress, within the limits and potentialities of the cultural construction of thought and feeling.[43]

As previously identified, Haynes's approach to identity formations – including his own queerness – has been shaped by his exposure to postmodern and post-structuralist theories which challenge the sanctity of 'the self' as a stable entity with an innate essence. He has explored this idea thematically in most, if not all, of his films. In the previous section of this chapter, I argued that the extensive simulation of Sirk in *Far from Heaven* works as a de-authorisation strategy that undercuts Haynes's status as the movie's 'auteur' and controlling force. Similarly, the level of pastiche on display in the movie is of a degree only perhaps matched by that in *Velvet Goldmine* and *I'm Not There* – and possibly exceeding both of them. As with simulation, pastiche troubles some audiences and critics as it 'de-authors' a piece of work, the mobilisation of quotations and references threatening to block out the creator's distinctive voice. But for a filmmaker who 'feels marginal', such employment of pastiche, as Dyer notes, merely chimes with and reflects 'what life is like'. In *Far from Heaven*, then, the widespread use of pastiche is a specifically political tactic, serving as an additional layer of confrontation and challenge to the persistence of specific models of attributing authorship and authority.

Conclusion

This chapter has engaged with a number of discussions and arguments relating to film authorship. After outlining an auteurist reading of *Far from Heaven* that connected the film to others in Haynes's œuvre, subsequent sections explored how the film's employment of strategies of simulation and pastiche – both of which it marshals extensively – significantly challenge authorial approaches to its content and form.

So pervasive are the terms 'simulation' and 'pastiche' in reviews, articles and theoretical essays on *Far from Heaven* that it is tempting also to read the film through other associated and connected terms. For example, rather than a simulation of Douglas Sirk films, might *Far from Heaven* more correctly be an adaptation of them? Alternatively, can Haynes's film be productively conceptualised as a remake or as a work of translation? Might it even be feasible to look at *Far from Heaven* as a piece of forgery, wilfully attempting to deceive its audience? (Indeed, were any viewers of Haynes's film so baffled by his imitation of Sirk that, like Baudrillard's mis-recognition of *The Last Picture Show*, they thought they were watching an actual film from the 1950s?) Adopting any of these terms and approaches – adaptation, remake, translation, forgery – would complicate understandings of *Far from Heaven*'s authorship yet further.

And yet, for all of its simulation of Sirk's style, and its borrowings from a broad range of other films, *Far from Heaven* contains unique and distinctive elements. It attacks auteurism but remains 'a Todd Haynes film'. This tension between repetition and innovation, as we will see in the next chapter, is also crucial for comprehending *Far from Heaven*'s resuscitation of melodrama as a generic form.

3. Genre

Compared to all of Todd Haynes's other films to date, *Far from Heaven* is the most straightforwardly generic. *Assassins* (1985) deconstructs the 'period biopic', in a manner redolent of Derek Jarman's film about *Caravaggio* (1986). As I have argued elsewhere, *Superstar: The Karen Carpenter Story* (1987), despite its short running time, is indebted to a range of generic forms, including star biopics, disaster movies, documentary, horror, and 'disease of the week' made-for-TV movies.[1] *Poison* (1991) has three separate narrative strands, each shot in a different idiom. The television short *Dottie Gets Spanked* (1993), made as part of the PBS series 'TV Families', is a period drama set in the 1950s, but one ruptured by perverse avant-garde dream sequences. *Safe* (1995) melds horror and melodrama in a form influenced by Kubrick, Antonioni, Akerman and others. The mixture of styles in *Velvet Goldmine* (1998) – social realism, pop promo, fantasy and science fiction, amongst others – is especially complex, as is that embodied in the multiple threads of *I'm Not There* (2007). In contrast, *Far from Heaven* is 'merely' a melodrama: specifically, a family melodrama indebted to those made in the 1950s for Universal by Douglas Sirk. Though Haynes had experimented with the effects of melodrama in *Superstar* and *Safe*, *Far from Heaven* is marked by a surprisingly rigorous adherence to the formal and narrative constraints of the genre. Indeed, for those viewers who had been following Haynes's career since his early controversial works, the lack of genre mixing in *Far from Heaven* may have seemed like a pointed move away from one of his most recognisable traits. And given that *Far from Heaven* was Haynes's first film made with partial support from the studios, some audiences may have asked: does the move into a more mainstream form of filmmaking necessitate the loss of an experimental approach to genre?

Of course, one of the main aims of this book is to demonstrate the richness and complexity of *Far from Heaven*, despite its 'straightforwardness'.

As the previous chapter argued, for instance, the film's employment of strategies of simulation and pastiche challenge traditional understandings of film authorship – and, in particular, the notion of Todd Haynes as an auteur with a recognisable stylistic 'stamp'. In this chapter, the decision by Haynes to recreate a 1950s melodrama is explored in more detail. The discussion is divided into four sections. The first identifies some of the main components of melodrama as a film genre, and the ways in which these are replicated, adhered to or modified by *Far from Heaven*. The second situates Haynes's film in relation to a number of others released in the first few years of the new century that can also be categorised as 'melodramas', and posits explanations for why this flurry of interest in the form occurred at this time. One major effect of the appearance of these melodramas, I will argue, is that they reveal how the array of genres on offer to audiences – and the emotional experiences they make available to their viewers – changes swiftly over time. The third section pays closer attention to those emotional experiences; it concentrates on the relationship between *Far from Heaven* and crying. Space is devoted to the mechanics and tactics employed by Haynes in order to elicit tears from audiences, including structures of knowledge, timing, empathy, identification and pathos. In addition, I explore the experience of watching actors weep on screen, and the impact this has on the 'realism' of a melodrama. Finally, following on from the recognition that many of the directors responsible for making screen melodramas in the early twenty-first century are gay/queer, and as a prelude to the last chapter of this book which explores the queerness of *Far from Heaven*, the final section of this chapter examines the long-standing relationship between melodrama and gay men.

Drawing the Parameters

Unlike other film genres, such as the western, melodrama is difficult to define clearly. Across the theoretical approaches to melodrama found in Film Studies literature, writers disagree on whether it is fundamentally a genre, a style, a sensibility or something else entirely. Partly, this is because melodrama has a lengthy and complex history. Thomas Elsaesser, for instance, identifies a broad array of cultural forms which fed into the development of film melodrama, including 'the late medieval morality play, the popular *gestes* and other forms of oral narrative and drama, like fairy-tales and folk-songs', as well as 'the romantic drama which had its heyday after the French Revolution and subsequently furnished many of the plots for operas, but which is itself unthinkable without the eighteenth-century sentimental novel'.[2] Certainly, a number of theorists have identified specific components of these examples (and others) which have connections with contemporary understandings of melodrama. Christine Gledhill, for example, has noted how eighteenth-century sentimental theatre placed an emphasis on spectacle, '*performance* traditions such as dumb show, pantomime, harlequinade, tumbling, acrobatics and balladry', and music as a 'non-verbal dimension of meaning'.[3] These three elements have significance for, and resonate with, film melodrama, as will be explored shortly.

In relation to the history of cinema, an additional complexity arises: melodrama has been used as a relatively flexible and porous category, applied to a broad array of individual films, many of which may not seem to sit easily with contemporary understandings of the term. Ben Singer, for instance, writing about silent film melodramas of the 1900s and 1910s, notes that,

As one quickly discerns from reading newspaper reviews and magazine essays from this period, the term's crucial, defining connotation in this period related not to pathos and heightened emotionality but rather to elements essentially antithetical to . . . domestic melodramas – action, thrilling sensationalism and physical violence.[4]

Similarly, Steve Neale, in an article focusing in particular on American studio output in the period 1938 to 1960, has identified how the term 'melodrama' was utilised by production companies to denote action thrillers with fast-paced storylines, episodic narratives, stunts and suspense, and populated by wicked villains, women in peril and daring heroes.[5] However, the dominant understanding of melodrama that developed within Film Studies in the 1970s, and which has inflected all subsequent theoretical discussions, does not feature these sorts of examples. Rather, it concentrates on a specific set of films which could be termed 'family melodramas' or 'maternal melodramas'. The key examples discussed – the melodrama canon – were produced by the major American film studios in the 1930s, 1940s and 1950s, and would include such titles as *Stella Dallas* (Vidor, 1937), *Letter from an Unknown Woman* (Ophüls, 1948), *Rebel Without a Cause* (Ray, 1955), *Some Came Running* (Minnelli, 1958) and several of Sirk's films, especially *All That Heaven Allows* (1955) and *Written on the Wind* (1956). It is this particular form of melodrama that *Far from Heaven* is indebted to, and which therefore deserves exploration.

The Hollywood 'classical melodramas' had a recognisable narrative form, style and tone. Aspects of this format were drawn from previous examples of melodrama – in film, and also in other forms of culture. Here, I want to outline four key aspects of the classical 'family melodrama'. In relation to each of these elements, I will offer a brief examination of their employment by *Far from Heaven*, and thus the ways in which Haynes's film fits with (or challenges) the generic template.

The first element which binds together many instances of the classical studio melodrama is narrative form, and the components from which it is constituted. Indeed, genres or sub-genres are often primarily defined by their repetition of similar narrative elements (with room for minor variations, of course). As the term 'family melodrama' implies, the films that make up this genre regularly focus on the conflicts and antagonisms within affluent or upwardly mobile middle-class families, and in particular on the individual emotional ordeals experienced by specific characters. Thomas Elsaesser has noted the combination of affluent locale and emotional drama that characterises the genre:

Melodrama is iconographically fixed by the claustrophobic atmosphere of the bourgeois home and/or the small-town setting, its emotional pattern is that of panic and latent hysteria, reinforced stylistically by a complex handling of space in interiors . . . to the point where the world seems totally predetermined and pervaded by 'meaning' and interpretable signs.[6]

Rebel Without a Cause, Written on the Wind, The Reckless Moment (Ophüls, 1949) and *Imitation of Life* (Sirk, 1959), for example, all adhere to this template.

Despite the focus on the family, examples of the classical melodrama usually feature a central protagonist. As Mercer and Shingler note, this individual

tends to be privileged by a high degree of audience identification. In this way, the audience is invited (or, indeed, induced) to sublimate their own fears and anxieties onto the central figure who is, in most cases, also the victim of the drama. This figure could either be the son, daughter or the mother but almost never a father. In fact, it is the father who tends to remain throughout these films the most unsympathetic figure, even more so when absent or deceased.[7]

That the protagonist is also a victim is crucial to the narrative and emotional dynamics of melodrama. As Haynes himself notes, unlike more respected dramatic forms that hinge on catharsis and break-through, classic melodrama is not about overcoming. The women in these films never transcend their conditions, either in thought or in deed. Rarely are we even sure what it is they learn from their struggles.[8]

The same point is emphasised by Elsaesser:

The family melodrama . . . often records the failure of the protagonist to act in a way that could shape the events and influence the emotional environment, let alone change the stifling social milieu. The world is closed, and the characters are acted upon. Melodrama confers on them a negative identity through suf-fering, and the progressive self-immolation and disillusionment generally ends in resignation: they emerge as lesser human beings for having become wise and acquiescent to the ways of the world.[9]

The identification of suffering and resignation as a repetitive configura-tion also relates to a final narrative feature worthy of note: the way in which melodramatic film narratives conclude. Regularly, instances of the genre end negatively or pessimistically, with protagonists left isolated, emotionally scarred and bereft. When positive conclusions do occur, as with *Magnificent Obsession* and *All That Heaven Allows*, for instance, these often happen swiftly, and fail to eradicate the memory and emotional impact of the suffering experienced and endured throughout the course of the narrative. Indeed, these upbeat endings are sometimes patently ironic and fake; the image of the deer in the snow that appears near the conclusion of *All That Heaven Allows*, a hyperbolic staged depiction of nature idealised, serves to undercut the narrative emphasis on Cary and Ron's attainment of heterosexual union.

Far from Heaven fits the typical classical melodrama narrative template to a significant degree, with some clear differences. The story focuses on a financially well-off family (they can afford a maid and a gardener; Cathy has her own car) living in the leafy suburbs. The claustropho-bia of the town of Hartford – expressed most clearly in the fact that the border between Cathy's public and private realms is never clearly demarcated, and in the circulation of vicious gossip that ruins her rela-tionship with Raymond – causes significant emotional turmoil. Cathy is the film's main character, a mother under tremendous strain to main-tain appearances. She is positioned throughout as a victim: unaware of her husband's homosexuality; the object of (largely unfounded) scandal-ous town rumour; naïvely liberal about racial difference, and thus at odds with the racism endemic in Hartford; and so on. At the film's end she has lost her husband to another man, her best friend Eleanor has given her the cold shoulder due to her relationship with Raymond, and he has departed for Baltimore. She has been publicly ostracised due to the rumours, and is left with the children and no income.

Contrary to the standard model of the classical melodrama, Cathy's husband Frank is not unsympathetic. This may in part be due to Haynes's personal investment in incorporating a gay storyline into *Far from Heaven*; it may also have been affected by negative test screenings of early cuts of the film. Finally, in line with Haynes's and Elsaesser's comments, the movie does not have a happy ending: Cathy waves goodbye to Raymond at the train station, and then gets into her car and drives away. A planned voiceover for this sequence was cut by Haynes, in order to make the impact 'more poignant and devastating'.[10] In doing so, the film's downbeat conclusion is comparable with those of *Stella Dallas* or *Letter from an Unknown Woman*.

Secondly, music is central to the operations of melodrama. The term 'melodrama' combines the Greek terms '*melos*' and '*drama*', the former meaning 'music'. As Thomas Elsaesser notes,

In its dictionary sense, melodrama is a dramatic narrative in which musical accompaniment marks the emotional effects. This is still perhaps the most useful definition, because it allows melodramatic elements to be seen as constituents of a system of punctuation, giving expressive colour and chromatic contrast to the story-line, by orchestrating the emotional ups and downs of the intrigue.[11]

Within classical film melodrama, the orchestral score (and it is almost always provided by a full orchestra) often fills in the gaps when words fail the characters or they are prevented from expressing their feelings. Certainly, the melodramatic score shares characteristics with those composed for many other types of Hollywood films: it can enhance audience identification with characters, smooth transitions between scenes, and contribute towards the drama of particular moments; musical themes may be associated with individual characters or specific relationships. Notably, however, the idiom of many melodramatic scores is derived from the nineteenth-century tradition of romantic music, with its emphasis on emotional expression, melody, dramatic contrasts in pitch and dynamics, and recurrent themes.

The score for *Far from Heaven* was composed by Elmer Bernstein; it was the last feature film he worked on before his death in 2004.

Bernstein composed for the movies consistently for over five decades, turning his hand to a broad range of genres, including biblical epics (*The Ten Commandments*, 1956), melodrama (*Some Came Running*), westerns (*The Magnificent Seven*, 1960; *True Grit*, 1969), comedy (*Airplane!*, 1980) and period drama (*The Age of Innocence*, 1993; *Devil in a Blue Dress*, 1995). Haynes was keenly aware of the importance of music within classical Hollywood melodrama. As Bernstein has commented, 'Todd had music in mind when he shot the film. He had made room for music. He wanted music to be an engine in this film, that the score should be a romantic score, that the score should be unashamed.'[12] In fact, Haynes used Bernstein's score for *To Kill a Mockingbird* (1962) – another film about racist attitudes in small-town America – as his scratch music when shooting *Far from Heaven*.[13] Bernstein's completed score has conventional elements seen across a range of genres: Cathy and Raymond have a theme, which is repeated, inflected in different styles; the dramatic scene in which Raymond's daughter is pursued by three bullies is enhanced with 'chase music'. However, the debt to classical melodrama is also clear. The opening credits are accompanied by a lushly melodic, sweeping piece of music that could have been used for some of Sirk's films, its movement between quiet and loud sections implying the emotional ups-and-downs of the narrative to come. In addition, moments of confrontation when characters struggle to express themselves – such as Cathy and Frank's failure to have sex after the party they host – are heightened, made stylistically excessive, through the addition of dramatic score.

This 'excess' is, indeed, a third key element of classical Hollywood melodrama. As Geoffrey Nowell-Smith has identified, the narrative form of the melodrama struggles to contain the emotional pressures and upheavals experienced by the lead characters:

The laying out of the problems 'realistically' always allows for the generating of an excess which cannot be accommodated. The more the plots press towards a resolution the harder it is to accommodate the excess. What is characteristic of the melodrama . . . is the way the excess is siphoned off. The undischarged emotion which cannot be accommodated within the action, subordinated as it is to the demands of family/lineage/inheritance, is traditionally expressed in the music and in the case of film, in certain elements of the *mise-en-scène*. That is to say, music and *mise-en-scène* do not heighten the emotionality of an element of the action: to some extent they substitute for it.[14]

This arguably reaches its apotheosis in several films made by Douglas Sirk, especially *All That Heaven Allows*, *Written on the Wind* and *Imitation of Life*. Cary's emotional turmoil in *All That Heaven Allows* is rarely expressed directly, but is captured by the design of her home: striking blocks of bright colour in warm/cold contrasts, mirrors and windows that closely frame her face, and (most obviously) the television set that is bought as a substitute for her relationship with her gardener, Ron. *Far from Heaven*'s production design works with a similar aesthetic of excess: warm and cold colours often boldly segregate parts of the frame; individual props (a framed picture of Cathy and Frank, a branch given to Cathy by Raymond) are over-determined in their significance, while others oppressively crowd the screen, contributing to the film's sense of claustrophobia.

Music is central to melodrama's sense of excess. As Barbara Klinger writes, 'critical moments in classic melodramas are usually accompanied by dramatic music that is so emphatic that it appears naïvely exaggerated.'[15] Discussing *Written on the Wind*, she isolates two key scenes – a swelling of strings as Marylee (Dorothy Malone) weeps against a tree, and the same character's wild dance to a jazz track whilst her father suffers a heart attack – as characteristic of classical melodrama's musical excesses. With *Far from Heaven*, Haynes wrote numerous musical cues into the film's script: 'Music bathes the shadowy quiet'; 'Music booms, sweeping us inexorably forward,' and so on.[16] Although Elmer Bernstein's score is less exaggerated than that of many classical instances of the genre, there are also sequences – Cathy walking in on Frank kissing another man in his office, Cathy and Raymond's separation outside of the Ritz cinema – whose emotional significance is underlined by an emphatic employment of strings, brass and/or piano.

Fourthly, and related to this sense of excess, melodrama is often positioned in relation to, or distinction from, realism. This affects not just the classical Hollywood melodramas but also, much more broadly, other incarnations of the form. Christine Gledhill argues that the perceived segregation between realism and melodrama occurred around the time of the birth of cinema in the late 1800s:

Recovery of realism and tragedy at the turn of the century as categories demarcating high from popular culture coincided with a re-masculinisation of cultural value. Realism came to be associated with (masculine) restraint and underplaying. It eschewed flamboyant characterisation in favour of psychological analysis, carried in verbal discourse and dialogue. The gestural rhetoric of melodramatic acting was displaced by 'naturalist' performance styles. The tragedy and realism focused on 'serious' social issues or inner dilemmas, recentring the hero and claiming tragic value for the failure of heroic potential. Sentiment and emotiveness were reduced in significance to 'sentimentality' and exaggeration, domestic detail counted as trivia, melodramatic utopianism as escapist fantasy and this total complex devalued by association with a 'feminised' popular culture.[17]

This conceptual split certainly helps to explain the low position of melodrama as a cultural form throughout much of the twentieth century (and subsequently); its association with domestic narratives, escapism, and women as protagonists and audiences contributed to its denigrated status. And many of the emblematic examples of the classical melodrama (*All That Heaven Allows*, say, or *Rebel Without a Cause*) fit within Gledhill's characterisation of the genre: they are marked by a hyperbolic style, a narrative focus on the family and domestic settings, outlandish plot elements, and so on.

However, despite the perseverance of the antinomy, the segregation between realism and melodrama is far from clear-cut or straightforward. 'Realism' is a complex concept, referring to a system of representational codes that regularly shift and re-align in relation to changing historical, cultural and technical understandings of how best to depict 'the real'. In addition, there are different forms of realism; a film's style and aesthetics may be distinct from those deemed to be realistic, but the characters may behave in emotionally realistic ways.[18] Further, classical Hollywood melodrama may be able to incorporate realistic elements, or insinuate a broader realistic structure beyond the frame of the characters which impinges on the film's events. As Thomas Elsaesser has argued,

the melodrama, at its most accomplished, seems capable of reproducing more directly than other genres the patterns of domination and exploitation existing in a given society, especially the relation between psychology, morality and class-consciousness, by emphasising so clearly an emotional dynamic whose social correlative is a network of external forces directed oppressively inward, and with which the characters themselves unwittingly collude to become their agents.[19]

Far from Heaven may, at first glance, seem like an unrealistic confection, a perception enhanced by its simulation of the style of certain 1950s films. And yet it contains elements that make it more 'realistic' than the movies it references. External sequences, for instance, were largely shot on location and not on artificial studio sound stages. Unlike the films of Douglas Sirk, the real world occasionally intrudes, as for instance when the Whitakers watch a television news broadcast. Beyond this however, the suffering of the protagonist in *Far from Heaven*, like those of many a classical melodrama, is clearly caused by wider structural problems – the status of race relations in America in the 1950s, for instance – that relate to the real world of the audiences watching. And it is this relationship – between the individual melodramatic movie and the context of its production and reception – that is the focus of the next section of this chapter.

'Why melodrama now?'

In an interview with Haynes that appeared in *L.A. Weekly* in 2002, Ella Taylor opened by observing: 'Todd Haynes is reeling from a weekend at the mercy of 60 junketeering journalists with but one question on their minds: Why melodrama now?'[20] The question is a valuable one, as it enables a critical exploration of the intentions, influences and antici-pated effects that underpin the production of a Sirkian homage in the first years of the twenty-first century. Haynes, of course – as discussed in Chapter 2's consideration of auteurism – had previously directed films inspired by, or related to, the workings of melodrama. Both *Superstar* and *Safe*, though hybrid texts, experimented with stylistic and narrative devices typically associated with the genre. *Far from Heaven*, although densely intertextual, is solidly generic in its simulation of the style Sirk perfected in his best-known 1950s films for Universal.

However, even after taking into account his history, Haynes's film raised particular concerns for commentators at the time of its release. Why revive this particular style? Was this merely a formal exercise or was there a more significant intention? More broadly, why did the melo-drama seem to be making a re-appearance on cinema screens, from a group of gay/queer directors? *Far from Heaven* was released around the same time as *The Deep End* (McGehee/Siegel, 2001), *Moulin Rouge!* (Luhrmann, 2001), *The Hours* (Daldry, 2002), *8 Women* (Ozon, 2002) and *Talk to Her* (Almodóvar, 2002), and a number of critics and journal-ists drew comparisons between Haynes's film and one or more of these other titles.[21] In this section of this chapter, I want briefly to consider three approaches to Haynes's film, and the timing of its production and release: that it serves to comment on changes in the 'family melodrama' and movies made for women; that it reveals the emotional force of particular modes of storytelling, and how these may be lost to history; and that it comments on, or relates to, American politics of the early twenty-first century.

Far from Heaven can be seen, in recreating the form of the 1950s family melodrama, as inviting audiences to reflect on how and why particular ways of telling stories in the movies become outmoded and disappear. Witnessing familiar actors such as Julianne Moore and Dennis Quaid exchange the mannered dialogue of an earlier form of cinema only heightens an awareness of the Sirkian style as archaic. Spectators may struggle to identify recent films that serve as contemporary incarnations of, say, *Written on the Wind*. As Richard Dyer observes of *Far from Heaven*,

At a minimum, anyone would recognise that the film does not work in the ways other recent films do that deal with domestic dramas, not glossy late women's films (*The Mirror Has Two Faces* 1994, *Waiting to Exhale* 1995), not understated semi-independents (*You Can Count On Me* 2000, *In the Bedroom* 2001, *The Shipping News* 2001), not heritage style (*The End of the Affair* 1999, *The Hours* 2002), not problem-of-the-week made-for-tv movies, not soap opera.[22]

Indeed, historical accounts of melodrama often suggest that, following a peak of popularity in the 1950s, the register and preoccupations of classical studio instances of the genre were transposed to television. The rhythms and narrative dynamics of soap opera – empathetic female characters as figures of identification, regular emotional outbursts, unexpected and outlandish plot developments, cliffhangers, claustrophobic and artificial domestic settings – can certainly be comprehended in relation to earlier forms of melodrama. And yet other elements of soap opera, such as the large cast of characters and the open-ended nature of the narrative, mark the form as distinct from the self-contained studio movie.

In 2002, a number of films were released into cinemas which could possibly be categorised as melodramas, including *The Banger Sisters*, *Crossroads*, *Divine Secrets of the Ya-Ya Sisterhood*, *Maid in Manhattan*, *My Big Fat Greek Wedding*, *Swept Away*, *Two Weeks Notice* and *A Walk to Remember*. These movies thus deserve comparison with Haynes's film – and, more importantly, the classical films upon which *Far from Heaven* draws. As with studio melodramas of the 1950s, these 2002 movies were all specifically marketed to a female demographic (although in both periods, a range of different tactics were employed in selling such films to both men and women, in order to attempt to maximise their potential audience). Unlike classical melodrama, however, many of these later films are comedic (some, such as the Madonna vehicle *Swept Away*, unintentionally so). In addition, some of the 2002 films – *Crossroads*, *Divine Secrets* – concentrate on groups of female friends, rather than the familial relations that predominate in 1950s examples.

From this list, arguably only *A Walk to Remember* (directed by Adam Shankman) can be categorised as a formulaic and generic melodrama. The film, based on the novel by Nicholas Sparks and a vehicle for teen starlet Mandy Moore, has a classically melodramatic narrative, complete with downbeat ending. Teenagers Landon (Shane West) and Jamie (Moore) meet and fall in love, but she is revealed to have leukaemia and has stopped responding to treatment. The pair get married; she eventually dies. This plot, centred on a relationship doomed by ill health, is clearly indebted to *Love Story* (Hiller, 1970); terminal illness has been utilised as a plot device in a lineage of screen melodramas that includes *Dark Victory* (Goulding, 1939), *Terms of Endearment* (Brooks, 1983), *Beaches* (Marshall, 1988) and *Dying Young* (Schumacher, 1991). *A Walk to Remember*'s dialogue is often directly constructed to provoke an emotional effect: after Jamie's death, for instance, Landon tells her father that he wishes he could have granted Jamie's desire to see a miracle. Her father replies that Jamie *did* indeed witness one: 'It was you,' he says. (Obviously, the individual viewer's affective response to this line could be either tears or nausea.) It is notable that, although the film is set in the present day, the narrative of the original novel takes place in the 1950s. In other words, the adaptation of the film had the potential to maintain the period setting and experiment with film style in a manner that would have made the film more directly comparable with *Far from Heaven*.

There is, in fact, an argument to be made that Nicholas Sparks is a crucial figure in keeping alive the narrative form of the classical film melodrama. The films based on his books – which also include *Message in a Bottle* (Mandoki, 1999), *The Notebook* (Nick Cassavetes, 2004), *Nights in Rodanthe* (Wolfe, 2008) and *Dear John* (Hallström, 2010) – are all unironic heterosexual romances in which the lead characters have to confront obstacles that block their union, such as war or grief. Both *The Notebook* and *Dear John* were extremely successful at the box office, suggesting a sizeable market for melodramatic narratives. However, the fact that the films based on Sparks's novels are unironic and stylistically unremarkable serves as a significant difference from the melodramatic films of Sirk, Ray, Minnelli and others. The critique of the family and the oppressive conservative forces of the affluent middle classes on show in such Sirk titles as *All That Heaven Allows* and *Written on the Wind* is absent from the Sparks films. Placing *Far from Heaven* alongside a film like *A Walk to Remember*, then, only serves to emphasise how much has been lost when a particular mode of filmmaking dies out. Traces of that form may persist, whereas others disappear. Excessively stylised mise-en-scène, for instance, is rarely seen in contemporary Hollywood studio dramas. When it does appear, as in Peyton Reed's *Down with Love* (2003), which mimics the style of 1960s Rock Hudson/Doris Day comedies, the impact is almost always solely aesthetic, rather than ironic or critical.

The second argument to make here is closely related to that just outlined. *Far from Heaven* and the other melodrama-referencing films released in the first years of the new century invited contemplation of the disappearance – or partial persistence – of the genre. However, some of them also prompted reflection on the emotional experiences associated with immersion in particular types of narratives, and how such experiences may become lost to the past. Melodramatic films, especially those made by Hollywood studios during the classical era, have often been pejoratively referred to as 'tearjerkers'. The implication behind the term is that the emotional response solicited by such movies is artificially and mechanically induced. Through the employment of such devices as the construction of empathetic characters, manipulative narrative structures and romantic music, directors can coerce tears from spectators. Such a critique, of course, fails to recognise the pleasure that many spectators may experience in being made to weep. (Steve Neale has explored in detail the mechanics used by filmmakers to solicit tears, and the pleasures this can provide for some audience members; I will discuss his arguments in the next section of this chapter.) But if *Far from Heaven* or *Moulin Rouge!* emotionally moved their audiences, then how does this reflect on contemporary cinema viewing more broadly?

Far from Heaven can, in fact, be seen as a scientific experiment in spectator response, with paying audiences as guinea pigs. Sirk's films, it can be assumed, made a sizeable number of their viewers cry – when Helen (Jane Wyman) recovers her sight at the conclusion of *Magnificent Obsession*, for instance, or when Annie Johnson (Juanita Moore) dies at the end of *Imitation of Life*, her rebellious daughter Sarah Jane remorsefully throwing herself on the coffin and begging for forgiveness. If Sirk's style and a narrative structure borrowed from melodrama were faithfully reconstituted, as Haynes attempted, would it have a similar impact on a contemporary audience? (A less expensive and time-consuming version of this experiment can be imagined: can a twenty-first-century spectator, perhaps especially one unfamiliar with cinema history, still be moved to tears by one of Sirk's films from the 1950s?)

Of course, Haynes was not merely conducting a $14 million experiment in emotional stimulation. Rather, if *Far from Heaven* is experienced as emotionally moving, it should provoke audience reflection. What is it about this linear narrative structure, the excessive mise-en-scène, the performances, and so on, that produced the emotional impact? How is being moved by this film different to being moved by a film set in the present day? Is one more effective than the other – and if so, why? How often are audiences moved by contemporary cinema? Manohla Dargis, in her review of *Far from Heaven*, argued that Julianne Moore's performance was central to the emotional power of the film. She went on to observe that 'Most filmmakers are no longer interested in making us cry; they want us to shiver, to shake, to jump in our seats or watch impassively as another one bites the dust. Have we become afraid to cry?'[23] This question is a significant one, as it suggests that film spectators of the early twenty-first century are rarely moved to tears in the auditorium, and that directors have become less interested in soliciting such a response. *Far from Heaven*, in its ability to move its audiences, encourages such a recognition.

For Daniel Mendelsohn, the widespread lack or distrust of emotional honesty that Dargis identified is directly related to a pervasive culture of irony. He argued that the resurgence of melodrama in films including *Far from Heaven* and television programmes such as *Six Feet Under* (yet again, created by a gay man, Alan Ball) could mark an ending of sorts to – or at least, a concerted attack on – the routine adoption of irony as a shield or tactic. Further, he identified the historical significance of this response in relation to 9/11:

After at least two full decades of ironic pop culture, ironic intellectual discourse, post-this, post-that – during which a sense of been-there, done-that permeated every level of mass culture – it was as if we were all ironied out. September 11 was the catalyst for a change that was already in the works [. . .] It's no accident that the triumphant return of melodrama, a drama that shuns irony, is happening right now. If irony deadens feeling, melodrama can be thought of as a kind of emotional shock treatment – a useful way, for a public that has been in the habit of distancing itself from sincerity, to feel its way back to some kind of unabashed authenticity.[24]

I will return to the relationship between *Far from Heaven* and 9/11 shortly. However, Mendelsohn's argument is an important one in identifying that the emotional directness of Haynes's film, and the affective impact it had on many viewers, is largely lacking in contemporary American cinema. The film that intentionally makes audiences cry has become a rare commodity.

Finally, *Far from Heaven*'s appearance in cinemas in 2002 can be seen as a pointed intervention or commentary relating to particular aspects of American politics. As has already been identified, independent cinema is often overtly political in its content, and all of Haynes's previous films (however obliquely) had confronted specific political concerns. Melodrama's relationship to politics is more complex, however – and given the lengthy history of the genre, and the broad and diverse array of films that the term has been used to designate, this is perhaps not surprising. It could be argued that melodrama's emphases on hyperbole, emotions and narrative twists and coincidences prevent instances of the genre from connection and engagement with real-world politics. Indeed, as Christine Gledhill has identified, until the critical rehabilitation of some directors of the genre in the 1970s, many film scholars used the term 'melodrama' negatively, associating it with a lack of seriousness and political significance, and with mass entertainment rather than 'high culture'.[25] Alternatively, the genre's concentration on victims and underdogs and the tribulations they suffer may effectively shine a light on the experiences and social conditions of individuals normally cast into the margins of other genres of storytelling. Laura Mulvey, for instance, has argued that melodrama can operate as a 'safety valve' for exploring the contradictions and complexities of family, gender roles and sexual relations under patriarchy.[26]

In relation to the politics of melodrama, it is highly significant that Haynes used Sirk as his stylistic template. The substantial attention which has been paid to Sirk by film theorists, a critical interrogation which began in the 1970s, has often argued for the director's films as distinct from many other classical studio melodramas in their inclusion of social critique. This approach to Sirk was partly inaugurated by the director himself. In a book-length interview with Sirk conducted by

Jon Halliday, first published in 1971, the director contextualised his work in melodrama in relation to a history of tragedy, and argued that his aims were similar to authors such as Euripides and Shakespeare who worked within generic constraints to criticise the workings of their own societies.[27] Sirk described the various techniques and devices he employed – including the false happy ending, irony, an artificial and claustrophobic mise-en-scène, and recurrent themes such as blindness and impotence – in order to proffer a critique of the bourgeoisie and the nuclear family. Also in 1971, the theory journal *Screen* devoted an issue to Sirk, which included Fred Camper's 'The Films of Douglas Sirk', Jon Halliday's 'Notes on Sirk's German Films' and Paul Willemen's essay 'Distanciation and Douglas Sirk', amongst other contributions.[28] Jon Halliday and Laura Mulvey's edited collection *Douglas Sirk* (1972) reprinted some of the essays from the previous year's special edition of *Screen*, and contained new material, including a translation by Thomas Elsaesser of Fassbinder's 'Six Films by Douglas Sirk'.[29] *Monogram* published an issue centred on melodrama in 1972, which included Elsaesser's article 'Tales of Sound and Fury'.[30] The critical focus on Sirk continued in earnest throughout the decade. As Barbara Klinger notes,

In the latter part of the 1970s, Sirk criticism was published in *Screen*, *Movie*, *Framework*, *Positif*, *The Velvet Light Trap*, *Film Comment*, and a variety of other British, French, and U.S. sources. Sirk retrospectives and special screenings began in the United States, and interviews continued. The 'boom' period had established Sirk as a director worthy of discourse, an established value that subsequent critics repeatedly affirmed.[31]

Although Sirk was often singled out for special attention, critics writing during the 1970s also examined movies by other directors of melodrama, including Vincente Minnelli, Nicholas Ray and Max Ophüls, making connected arguments regarding their repetitively employed stylistic decisions and narrative tropes.[32] Of course, not all melodramatic films operate as critiques – coded or otherwise – of specific social conditions. But since Sirk's œuvre was first subjected to sustained theoretical scrutiny, melodrama as a film genre has often been recognised as a potential vehicle for exploring particular political concerns.

This political imperative was central to the creation of *Far from Heaven*, as Haynes has identified:

Creating a fifties-era melodrama today, smack in the midst of this pumped-up, adrenaline-crazed era, might seem a perplexing impulse. But it's my belief that contemporary audiences are in dire need of something to *do*, something to say in response to the perpetual, one-way onslaught of stimulus. To impose upon the seeming innocence of the 1950s themes as mutually volatile as race and sexuality is to reveal how volatile those subjects remain today – and how much our current climate of complacent stability has in common with that bygone era. So despite the script's allegiance to the formalities of its time, it must connect emotionally with a contemporary audience in order to succeed.[33]

That is, Haynes wanted to provoke reflection on the racism, sexism and homophobia of the 1950s, as well as to invite audiences to contemplate how much things have changed in the intervening decades. His depictions of the social and political conditions of the time are often fleeting, but informative. Frank is able to identify specific social spaces – the cinema, the gay bar – as meeting places for gay men. There is no evidence of the gay rights movements that were taking shape at the time in the United States, such as the Mattachine Society (formed in 1950), though – to be fair – such groups did tend to form around large cities such as Los Angeles, Chicago and New York. The racism of the citizens of Hartford is demonstrated. At the Whitakers' party, for example, one guest claims that 'there are no Negroes' in Connecticut; the shot cuts to two black serving staff, who have clearly heard his comment. Most obviously, Cathy's friendship with Raymond is configured as impossible. A broader context of race relations in America also briefly appears: Cathy is door-stepped by the NAACP; the Whitakers watch television news coverage of President Eisenhower ordering the army to enforce racial integration at Little Rock Central High School in Arkansas (which took place on 24 September 1957). Casual sexism is also on display, most evidently in Frank's comment at the Whitakers' party about Cathy's looks: 'Smoke and mirrors, fellas, that's all it is. You should see her without her face on!'

Of course, in the intervening decades, significant advances have been made in civil rights for women, gay men and lesbians, African-Americans, and other groups. However, full equality remains unattained. Just prior to the release of *Far from Heaven*, the dominant politics of the United States moved to the right. Democratic President Bill Clinton was ousted, and replaced in January 2001 by George W. Bush. Towards the end of Clinton's presidency, two violent murders – of forty-nine-year-old black man James Byrd, Jr, in Texas in June 1998, and of twenty-one-year-old white gay student Matthew Shepard in Colorado

in October of the same year – drew widespread attention to the persistence of racism and homophobia in the United States. Around the same
time, in relation to gay rights, the issues of same-sex unions and mar-
riages, adoption by same-sex couples, and gay men and lesbians serving
in the military continued to be politically divisive across North America.
With the Republican party returning to power, the critique in *Far from
Heaven* of oppressive conservative forces could be seen as a warning: the
1950s were not that long ago, and retrograde moves in tolerance and
acceptance of 'minority groups' are always feasible.

Indeed, in relation to this subject, one other possibility presents
itself: following on from Daniel Mendelsohn's argument above, is *Far
from Heaven* a 9/11 movie? Of course, given that the film went into pre-
production in 2000, the script was not intentionally about those events.
The movie was actually shot shortly after the destruction of the World
Trade Center. As Christine Vachon writes about the scenes filmed in
New York:

Far from Heaven is made in a war zone [. . .] Production is dead in New York right
now; everything has stopped – except us. We are the only game in town, so we
have all the top people manning our departments [. . .] Everybody is jumpy;
our days are punctuated by the wail of police sirens, anthrax alerts, and Code
Orange.[34]

In the wake of 9/11, American filmmakers struggled to ascertain what
audiences wanted to see at the cinema. Light and frothy escapist entertainment, such as romantic comedies? Spectacular scenes of destruction
that could be enjoyed as retributive and cathartic? The return to the
1950s that *Far from Heaven* presents can be seen as a form of escapism, an
opportunity to enjoy watching today's actors in a knowing recreation of
a film style from a different era. And yet the movie's representation of
a pervasive racism sits uncomfortably with the anti-Muslim sentiments
that spread across the United States after September 2001. Haynes's film
operates as a clear critique of racist attitudes and behaviours, and was
screened in American cinemas just as a fresh wave of antipathy, hatred
and suspicion towards non-white immigrants (and others) manifested.

Far from Heaven and Crying

As the previous section of this chapter suggested, it is feasible that one
of the causes behind the resuscitation of film melodrama in the early

twenty-first century, by Haynes and others, was the desire to demonstrate how cinema's ability to provoke emotional responses has changed. This may have had two related intentions: to demonstrate what used to move audiences at the cinema in the 1940s and 1950s, and how the mechanics of this have become outmoded, or at least historically distant; and to attempt to provoke a fresh wave of emotional responses from audiences, re-introducing them to the pleasures of weeping in public. What is notable in the critical and theoretical writings on *Far from Heaven* is the recurrence of confessions about crying – and reflective, analytical considerations of the experience of being moved by the film. In addition, in line with its generic replication of the family melodrama, there is a substantial amount of crying depicted in *Far from Heaven*. In this section of the chapter, then, I will explore in more detail the relationship between *Far from Heaven* and tears. In particular, space will be devoted to two main topics. Firstly, through the employment of which particular mechanics does Haynes's film have the ability to move audiences to tears? Steve Neale's arguments about timing and knowledge structures will be considered here, as will theories about pathos and empathy. Secondly, attention will be paid to the specifics of actors crying on screen: the pleasures for audiences of watching actors emote; how judgements are made regarding the authenticity of screen tears; and the problematic relationship between the artifice of melodrama and the 'realism' of actors' emotions.

Douglas Sirk, being interviewed by Jon Halliday, commented on working with producer Ross Hunter on *Magnificent Obsession*: 'He was always coming to me and saying, "Doug, Doug, make them weep! Please make them weep!" And every scene where I was trying to do something, he'd say, "I want 500 handkerchiefs to come out at this point." '[35] Haynes has stated that one of his main intentions with *Far from Heaven* was, like Sirk, to attempt to move his audience – even while he recognised that, paradoxically, the simulation of a Sirkian style could act as a barrier:

This film could so easily not have been emotionally enveloping for all the obvious reasons, and could have been considered just an interesting stylistic experiment in reference to another period that would have intrigued an intellectual crowd. But at the most basic level I wanted to make a movie that made people cry.[36]

For some audiences and reviewers, the film provoked laughter, rather than tears. As Haynes commented on one particular showing,

In Venice, there was a very well-attended press screening and we heard after-wards it was filled with a lot of appreciative laughter. I realised in the laughter, there is some interaction with the codes that we're obviously playing with – and ultimately embracing.[37]

Initial laughter could give way to other forms of emotional engagement, of course. Andrew O'Hehir, for instance, writing for *Salon*, observed that:

Far from Heaven is so intensely stylized you can't help feeling, at least at first, that some kind of ironic commentary is intended. It's only natural to giggle at the Magnatech ads, at the perfect Technicolor streets with their spotless arrays of Oldsmobiles and Plymouths, at the outrageous high-heeled pumps worn by Cathy's catty best friend (Patricia Clarkson, doing an uncanny impersonation of one of those Agnes Moorehead supporting roles) or at Moore's voluminous skirt in aquamarine satin, which looks as if you could camp a pack of Cub Scouts under it or convert it into parachutes in wartime [. . .] But Haynes is far too sophisticated (in a good way) to make derision his main instrument here. After you get over the sheer artificial plushness of the movie, you begin to notice that the characters – even though they're the artfully overdrawn types of '50s Hollywood – are experiencing real emotions.[38]

Other writers have been much more direct in admitting how the film could move audiences to tears, such as Manohla Dargis, quoted in the previous section of this chapter. Richard Dyer, in his analysis of the film, admits that

The first time I saw *Far from Heaven* . . ., there were moments when I could not see the screen for crying. On the other hand, I was fully conscious of the way the film was doing 1950s Hollywood melodrama, was pastiche [. . .] At a minimum, *Far from Heaven* is an especially strong vindication of the proposition that pastiche and emotion are not incompatible.[39]

Dyer's honest comment, then, neatly squares with Haynes's recognition that adopting or simulating an outmoded film style operates as a hurdle for spectators to overcome before (or at the same time as) emotional engagement occurs.

How do melodramas make their audiences cry? What techniques did Sirk and others employ to provoke viewers to grab for and moisten their '500 handkerchiefs'? And does *Far from Heaven* simply appropriate these techniques wholesale, or does it utilise additional tactics? A number of mechanics need to be considered here: the relationship between audience knowledge of plot developments and that of the characters in the fiction; the timing of narrative events; and empathy and identification with characters, including the workings of pathos.

One of the most sustained attempts to explain how melodrama provokes audiences to cry is Steve Neale's essay 'Melodrama and Tears', published in 1986. Neale notes that narrative structures in film melodrama regularly involve 'the production of discrepancies between the knowledge and point of view of the spectator and the knowledge and points of view of the characters, such that the spectator often *knows more*'.[40] The viewer can foresee how events are likely to unfurl but is unable to intervene, and has to watch helplessly from outside the realm of the story. It is this inability to influence the course of events that contributes to the solicitation of the spectator's tears. Neale quotes Franco Moretti: 'Tears are always the product of powerlessness. They presuppose two mutually opposed facts: that it is clear how the present state of things should be changed – and that this change is impossible.'[41] In addition, provoking tears from the viewer is centrally related to the timing of narrative events – specifically, the coming together of the knowledge of the viewer with that of the characters in the tale. As Neale writes,

Time in general and the timing of the coincidence of points of view in particular are indeed crucial – not that the coincidence is always too late (though it may be, of course), but rather that it is always *delayed*. Tears can come whether the coincidence comes too late or just in time, provided there is a delay, and the possibility, therefore, that it *may* come too late [. . .] We are dependent, not on time in the abstract, but on the time of the narrative and its narration. And the longer there is delay, the more we are likely to cry, because the powerlessness of our position will be intensified, whatever the outcome of events, 'happy' or 'sad', too late or just in time.[42]

Thus, in *Letter from an Unknown Woman*, viewers have observed Lisa's repeated attempts to garner Stefan's attention, and her sustained devotion to him despite his general ignorance of her existence. When Stefan finally pieces together from his memory his various encounters with Lisa, and the extent of her love for him, it is too late: she has died.

In relation to *Far from Heaven*, this concatenation of audience versus character knowledge, the narrative timing of information and revelations, and viewer powerlessness help to explain its audiences being emotionally moved. Indeed, Cathy is a victim to such devices twice over, in relation to both her husband's homosexuality and the town gossip about her relationship with Raymond. Viewers are privy to Frank's cruising in the cinema and his visit to a gay bar. Many will have picked up on the coded implications of his arrest for 'loitering' which occurs in the film's first minutes. Audiences have to wait for Cathy to discover that her husband is gay, and what impact this will have on their idealised family. The structure is echoed again, later in the narrative: audiences witness Frank pick up another man while he and Cathy are on holiday in Miami, a clear demonstration that the psychiatric treatment to 'cure' his homosexuality has not worked. Again, there is a delay before he confesses his love for this man to Cathy. (Whether audiences are moved by these scenes depends, of course, on their relationships with Cathy and Frank, and their attitudes to Frank's behaviour.) More significantly – as it directly echoes the narrative of *All That Heaven Allows* – Cathy's relationship with Raymond is swiftly established as likely to be doomed. Viewers observe Sybil watching Cathy and Raymond interact, with a look which clearly recognises their conversations as potentially inappropriate; later, the camera privileges Mona's chance spotting of the pair visiting Ernie's bar, her smirk insinuating the damage she will cause. Only after being ostracised at the ballet recital, and Eleanor informing Cathy that she is the focus of gossip, does Cathy break things off with Raymond. When Frank leaves Cathy, she is free to try to repair things with Raymond – but it is too late, as he has sold his business and intends to move to Baltimore. The closing train station scene offers the slim possibility that Raymond will change his mind, but too many forces conspire to keep the couple apart and Cathy can only mutely wave goodbye.

In addition to the combination of knowledge, timing and powerlessness, the provocation of audiences to tears by melodrama is also influenced by other factors. Musical score is key, for example. Simon Frith writes that, 'Music, it seems, can convey and clarify the emotional significance of a scene, the true, "real" feelings of the characters involved in it.'[43] The romantic music deployed in many melodramatic films may complement emotions expressed by the characters, or (as noted earlier) it may stand in for what they cannot say. The use of particular instruments – strings, woodwind, brass – characterises the 'emotive' score typical of classical melodrama, with specific types of melody (and, even more basically, chord progressions) symbolising emotions such as sorrow or grief, and/or evoking them in viewers. Exactly how audiences 'read' or understand a film's musical score has been explored by a number of authors, who differ in their opinions regarding whether particular forms of music have an innate ability to move listeners, or whether it is necessary for them to learn that, for instance, this chord progression denotes 'sadness'.[44] In *Far from Heaven*, Elmer Bernstein's score contributes significantly to the emotional impact of those scenes in which Cathy's status as a victim of circumstance is especially pronounced: as Frank confesses his love for another man, for instance, weeping in the Whitakers' front room; or at the train station, as Raymond leaves for Baltimore.

Further, the relationship between melodrama and tears necessarily operates in relation to the complex dynamics of empathy, identification and pathos. An audience's emotional response to *Far from Heaven* will be significantly affected by their spectatorial and affective relationship with Cathy. Empathy is often differentiated from sympathy: one feels empathy with someone else, but sympathy for them. Empathy, that is, involves a sharing of emotional states with another person. As Carl Plantinga puts it, 'Empathy consists of a capacity or disposition to know, to feel, and to respond congruently to what another is feeling, and the process of doing so.'[45] Although *Far from Heaven* could cause a spectator to weep who merely sympathises with Cathy's plight, the tears are likely to be more copious if there is an empathetic bond with the character. This may be further enhanced if the spectator has a personal investment in a particular actor or star, having followed their career. Empathy/ sympathy and identification with a character can be complicated by similar relations with an actor's star image – or the two may be largely mutually supportive. A spectator who is a fan of Julianne Moore, or who respects and highly rates the performances she has given in other films, may be more prone to emotional involvement with her character in *Far from Heaven*.

Pathos is a key emotional experience to consider in relation to melodrama, and the ability of the genre to make audiences cry. As Mary Ann Doane notes, in an essay on the operations of pathos in the cinema of Todd Haynes, 'The term *pathos* is derived from the Greek word for *suffering* or *deep feeling*.'[46] Pathos is engaged or provoked by melodrama due to the narrative centrality of characters who are victims: 'Pathos closely allies itself with the delineation of a lack of social power and effectivity characteristic of the cultural positioning of children and women (so frequently the protagonists of Haynes's films).'[47] Identification and empathy may involve or threaten to produce a (potentially troubling) breaking-down of the barrier between the spectator and the screen fiction, in which emotional congruence blurs the separation of the 'real' viewer from the 'constructed' character. As Doane points out, the same is true of pathos:

Pathos is a textual effect that implies a closeness, an immediacy, and hence an uncritical spectator – one who is taken in, often to the point of tears. It entails a loss or fading of subjectivity in the process of signification, full immersion in a discourse.[48]

It is this combination of elements – an uncritical spectatorial closeness involving immersive identification, a narrative concentration on victim characters, the provocation of weeping through pathos – that has previously contributed in part to the low cultural status of melodrama. Female fans of melodrama were denigrated as much as the genre itself for an emphasis on emotionality, 'negative feeling', and excessive identification between viewer and protagonist.

Certainly, this does raise a central concern in relation to melodrama and tears: why would film audiences want to subject themselves to an experience that will make them cry? A critical approach would suggest that viewers who enjoy crying at cinema are masochistic, taking vicarious pleasure in enduring someone else's pain, and responding with their own tears of frustration or sympathy at the protagonist's plight. Steve Neale, discussing viewers crying at a melodrama's conclusion, emphasises the frustration: 'Crying . . . is not just an expression of pain or displeasure of non-satisfaction. As a demand *for* satisfaction, it is the vehicle of a wish – a fantasy – that satisfaction is possible, that the object can be restored, the loss eradicated.'[49] A more positive perspective would argue for the cathartic, purging or pleasurable experience of crying at the cinema. Mary Beth Oliver, having conducted numerous interviews with women about weeping at the movies, highlighted that they regularly reported positive feelings about crying, attaining pleasure and satisfaction in tears induced by cultural texts.[50] Robyn Warhol has gone further, and argued for the political significance of 'having a good cry':

As I see it, the culture's lingering embarrassment over having a good cry is grounded partly in a gynophobic and homophobic reaction to the effeminate connotations of textually induced crying; partly in modernism's philosophical and aesthetic recoil from the feminine associations of popular culture itself, and

Figure 8 Cathy crying in *Far from Heaven* (© Focus Features/Vulcan Productions)

especially of sentimental popular culture; and partly in specifically modernist models of what crying does in and to the body of a reader.[51]

Todd Haynes's resuscitation of melodrama with *Far from Heaven* can be seen to contribute to the same political project. If crying at the cinema is a rare experience, his film seems to ask, is that due to wider cultural forces that have devalued or stymied such behaviour? *Far from Heaven* attempts, through the employment of tearjerking devices, to re-introduce cinema auditoria to the sound of noses being blown.

In addition to the crying of audiences of the film, there is a great deal of weeping up on the screen in *Far from Heaven*. Cathy sobs in the garden, attempting to hide behind a bush, after Eleanor notices the bruise on her forehead caused by Frank (see Figure 8). Later, a solitary tear runs from the corner of Cathy's right eye as she tells Raymond, outside the Ritz cinema, that they cannot be friends. Frank noisily breaks down in a chair, prompting his daughter Janice to cry, just before his confession to Cathy that finally brings their marriage to an end. When Cathy and Raymond talk outside his house at night and he admits he is moving to Baltimore, both of them cry. Towards the end of the film, Cathy lies across her bed and weeps, in a shot that references Max Ophüls's *The Reckless Moment*. All of this crying fits with the generic form of the classical melodrama, many examples of which feature moments of spectacular sobbing or stifled, shameful sniffling and blubbing; Sarah Jane's noisy and mournful wail at the conclusion of *Imitation of Life* serves as an illustration of the former, Cary's weeping at the mill when she tries to end her relationship with Ron in *All That Heaven Allows* a depiction of the latter.

Watching the characters cry in *Far from Heaven* raises a number of concerns about acting, authenticity, realism and audience viewing pleasures that are worth unpacking. The on-screen tears of actors can be produced by a range of methods. Ideally, of course, an actor's tears should result from their immersion in a character and narrative, their emotions a response to the staged situation that are as close as possible to those which would occur in real circumstances. Alternatively, an actor may draw on a previous personal experience of emotional hurt to induce their upset, transposing their emotion from one (real, past) scenario to another (filmed, present). If actors cannot induce crying, other film production tricks are available; the 'tear stick', dabbed beneath the eyes, consists of a combination of menthol and camphor, and will provoke actors to cry.

Audiences may be particularly judgemental when evaluating the ability of actors to cry on screen. Faked or invisible tears (a dry but crumpled face) may be laughable, unconvincing. 'Tear stick' tears are often overly tidy, single lines of liquid running neatly down the cheeks. Spectacular, snotty blubbing may look overly 'method'. The cinematic or televisual close-up enables audiences to scrutinise the faces of crying actors closely, and evaluate the authenticity of the emotion expressed. (Such shots also raise concerns about the sadism of directors, inducing emotion from actors and capturing it before a lens, and the affiliated sadism of spectators, who may be taking pleasure in watching an actor cry.) Because crying is associated with weakness and vulnerability, exposes the porous nature of the body in an unglamorous way, and can be difficult to control physically, actors who can cry in a convincing manner may be perceived as more skilled than others. While certain actors seem incapable of crying on screen, others (Kristen Bell, Matthew Fox, Naomi Watts, Julianne Moore) have established reputations as 'good criers'. In numerous interviews, Moore has been asked about crying on screen. She told Scott Tobias:

I can do it, but it doesn't mean that I like it. I do it because you're supposed to. That's what the part is. That's where the character goes at that moment. I kind of like the range of it. I like the enormous range of emotion that you can do on a film [. . .] When I was younger, I thought I had to shut myself off, work really hard to cry. I learned after a while that that's just not . . . You know, often in life, you cry when you're caught off-guard. That's where I need to be when I'm acting, too.[52]

Whilst almost all crying on screen in fictional movies is 'acting' – except, perhaps, that of some infants and children – certain types of performing emotion, those which are arguably 'most realistic', are evaluated more highly than others.

This is a significant topic in relation to *Far from Heaven* as the tears on display in the film are a marker of 'authenticity' in a text largely dominated by the artificiality of the Sirkian style. As was argued earlier, realism and melodrama are sometimes (incorrectly) seen as antithetical. In *Far from Heaven*, as in many examples of classical melodrama, the emotional impact of the film is dependent, to a substantial extent, on the tears of the cast. The meticulous and immaculate surface of the stylised décor, props, lighting, dialogue and performance style in *Far from Heaven* are ruptured somewhat by the 'realistic' tears of the actors. Dennis Haysbert's tears are minor, his eyes glistening in the dark as Raymond tells Cathy he is moving to Baltimore. When Frank tells Cathy he has fallen in love with another man, Dennis Quaid's tears occur somewhat hidden in blue or purple light. Accompanied by hands gnarled in anguish, words and phrases stammering out, sticky-mouthed, he sobs rather than weeps. Julianne Moore's tears are a constituent component of the film's spectacle. At times, they are clearly aestheticised: her crying on the bed, in which her face is obscured; the single immaculate tear she sheds outside the cinema. At others, though, the tears disavow or cut through the film's style. Outside Raymond's house, her eyes brim as she hopefully suggests that she could also move to Baltimore, her voice cracking as she says 'No one would know us there.' Later, on the phone to Frank, blue light catches the tears on her cheeks. 'You never could remember my carpool days', she says, her voice a little husky from the hurt, the emotional pain especially poignant for being contrasted with the quotidian.

Gay Men and Mainstream Melodrama

One of the main changes that Haynes made to the generic template of the classical or Sirkian melodrama was to introduce homosexuality into the narrative, in the form of Frank's plotline. And as was identified earlier in this chapter, he was only one of several gay/queer directors – including Stephen Daldry and Baz Luhrmann – who revitalised and experimented with the genre in the opening years of the twenty-first century. This invites further investigation: what exactly is the relationship between homosexuality and classical Hollywood melodrama? In this final section of this chapter, I want to explore two main topics. Firstly, consideration will be given to the queerness, or lack of, in classical melodramas of the 1940s and 1950s. Secondly, attention will be turned to the appeal of such films to gay male spectators.

There is almost no overt homosexuality depicted in American studio pictures produced in the 1940s and 1950s. This is largely due to the proscriptions contained within the Motion Picture Production Code – usually referred to as the Hays Code, after the name of its author, Will H. Hays. The Code was enforced from 1934 to 1968, affecting the vast majority of studio feature films. It was eventually abandoned in favour of the ratings system of the MPAA (Motion Picture Association of America). The Hays Code was not enforced by federal, state or city legislation; rather, it was adopted by Hollywood as a system of self-regulation, in the hopes of avoiding government legislation and censorship. Among the various topics banned or censored by the Code were references to alleged sex perversions (such as homosexuality) and depictions of miscegenation. In other words, if *Far from Heaven* had been made in the 1950s, both Frank's dalliances with other men and Cathy's relationship with Raymond would not have been allowed.

Of course, even with the prescriptive and censorious Code in place, homosexuality was not entirely eradicated from the screen. Indeed, it made itself felt or present through three particular systems or influences: codes of representation; the input of specific personnel; and blatant omission. Firstly, then, subtle systems of representation enabled characters to be depicted who, though not openly gay, were difficult to categorise as heterosexual. Coded aspects of costume, hair and make-up, vocal delivery and physical performance could all be used to insinuate 'non-heterosexuality'. To take just two examples: how are audiences to understand Mrs Danvers's (Judith Anderson) relationship with the second Mrs de Winter (Joan Fontaine) in *Rebecca* (Hitchcock, 1940), or Plato's (Sal Mineo) attachment to Jim Stark (James Dean) in *Rebel Without a Cause* (Ray, 1955)? Richard Dyer, in his book *The Matter of Images*, identifies several stereotypes used repeatedly to represent queerness on screen throughout cinema's history, including 'inbetween-ness' (that is,

feminine men and masculine women) and 'the sad young man'.[53] Mrs
Danvers and Plato serve as examples of these types, respectively.

Secondly, a large number of gay and lesbian personnel worked
in the film industry at the time – including in front of the camera –
sometimes leaving a queer trace on their films. This had a significant
influence on the movies of Douglas Sirk. Agnes Moorehead appeared
in *Magnificent Obsession* and *All That Heaven Allows*, cast as the best friend
of characters played by Jane Wyman. Rock Hudson worked on six films
with Sirk. Despite the latter often being cast as heterosexual romantic
lead, some authors claim that Hudson's homosexuality is evident in his
performances. As Laura Cottingham, for instance, writes:

> Decades after leaving Hollywood, Sirk confided to an interviewer that leading
> ladies routinely complained that Hudson wouldn't *really* kiss them, and that it
> took special direction to transform the man-loving Hudson into a mainstream-
> appropriate, heterosexual-acting film star. Careful viewing of *All That Heaven
> Allows* reveals that Hudson's face does not always look right. He is not really
> interested in Jane Wyman. He is not *acting* right.[54]

Similar arguments can be made about other stars who appeared in
melodramas, including James Dean, Montgomery Clift, Marjorie Main,
Sal Mineo and Barbara Stanwyck. Here, I do not want to suggest that
lesbian and gay actors can never convincingly 'play straight' – an argument which has recently been revived in relation to *Will and Grace* star
Sean Hayes. A large number of closeted actors continue to work in
Hollywood, being routinely cast in heterosexual roles. However, close
inspection and analysis of the performances of these actors can sometimes reveal a queer register or trace that exceeds the limitations of the
character as scripted.

Large numbers of queer people worked in the film industry during the
decades of the Hays Code, including producers, directors, script-writers,
production designers and wardrobe artists. There is not adequate space
here to consider all of these roles in detail; however, brief comment on
several key figures is worth making in order to provide a flavour of their
influence. The impact that a director's sexual orientation can have on
their films was considered in the previous chapter in relation to Todd
Haynes and his history of engagement with queer activism and politics.
Nicholas Ray, director of *Rebel Without a Cause*, was 'bisexual for most
of his life', according to Jonathan Rosenbaum, and invested male–
female and male–male 'pairings with similar erotic as well as romantic

dynamics'.[55] Ross Hunter, who produced seven of Sirk's films, including *All That Heaven Allows* and *Imitation of Life*, was gay. Sirk even suggested that Hunter had an influence on Rock Hudson's sexual orientation: 'I sometimes think Ross Hunter played a part in pushing Rock towards being homosexual. At first, Rock seemed to me to lie near the middle of the sexual spectrum, but when he met up with Ross, that was it.'[56] Finally, William Inge was a gay playwright; his play *Picnic* was made into a studio family melodrama in 1955 by Joshua Logan. Inge also wrote the screenplays of *Splendor in the Grass* (Kazan, 1961) and *All Fall Down* (Frankenheimer, 1962). As Jeff Johnson has argued, Inge's work is characterised by a subversive – arguably, queer – approach to gender and sexuality, in which stereotypes are challenged and gender roles reversed.[57]

Thirdly, the homosexuality in classical melodrama is often glaringly absent. Adapted books and plays lost (or had clumsily clouded) their gay/queer content in order to appease the Hays code. Viewers familiar with the source texts would be aware of the judicious pruning. *Tea and Sympathy* (Minnelli, 1956) is a toned-down adaptation of the 1953 stage play by Robert Anderson. Tom Lee (John Kerr) is a student at prep school who likes classical music, sewing and going to the theatre; he is bullied for his tastes by fellow pupils. The House Master's wife, Laura (Deborah Kerr), takes notice and pity, and befriends him; eventually the two have sex. It is unclear whether Tom is gay, his orientation 'cured' by Laura, or whether he is merely a heterosexual man with particular skills and hobbies. Similar obfuscation marks several films based on plays by Tennessee Williams, including *A Streetcar Named Desire* (Kazan, 1951), *Cat on a Hot Tin Roof* (Brooks, 1958) and *Suddenly, Last Summer* (Mankiewicz, 1959). (Ironically, Gore Vidal was employed to work on the screenplay of *Suddenly, Last Summer*, not necessarily the most appropriate choice of writer to 'de-homo' the original play.) The gaping holes left in these films, however, taken in tandem with the excesses of melodrama, may actually (counter to intention) have enhanced their queer character.

These factors all help to explain the relationship that some gay male spectators have historically had with melodrama. Stereotypically, gay audiences are often assumed to have an affinity with melodrama, as well as with the musical.[58] (There are, of course, links between the two genres, in the narrative centrality afforded to female protagonists and the emphasis placed on emotional expression.) A useful summary of the relationship between homosexuality and the melodrama is provided by Finch and Kwietniowski in their essay on *Maurice* (Ivory, 1987), and touches on some points already raised:

Gay men have always been associated with Hollywood melodrama, of course: narratively, not as subjects, but as symptoms, effects of disorder, most spectacularly in late classic melodramas like *Tea and Sympathy*, 1956, *Suddenly Last Summer*, 1959, *Reflections in a Golden Eye*, 1962; in terms of performance, as exaggerated, hysterical, unruly – Dean, Clift; as instrumental off-screen figures of the genre – George Cukor, Tennessee Williams – and, particularly, hairdressers, designers, costumiers – *gossips*; finally, as spectators, in terms of over-identification (Judy), imitation (Bette, Tallulah) – an empathy with melodrama's painful impossibilities, and also an ironic appreciation of the genre's excesses, or camp. In this sense, the subtext for a weepie is always homosexuality; *Maurice* is already massively over-determined.[59]

Three key terms or perspectives relating to gay men as audiences of melodrama are engaged here: excess, camp, and identification with female stars. Although these topics are intimately connected, they each deserve brief consideration.

As identified earlier in this chapter, one of the defining characteristics of many classical Hollywood melodramas is an excessive mise-en-scène and score, both of which may take on meaning and emotional force that cannot be contained by the narrative. Beyond these facets, other components of the studio melodrama of the 1940s and 1950s could be seen as 'excessive', including the performance styles of stars such as Lana Turner, Joan Crawford and Bette Davis, and the plot contrivances and narrative twists. Mercer and Shingler have suggested that these excesses appealed to gay male audiences:

Films like Sirk's, as well as examples from the oeuvres of Minnelli, Ray, Cukor, Wilder and Losey, achieved cult status within the gay subculture as a direct consequence of the very excessiveness, extreme emotionality, mannered performances, style and very direct sentimental form of address that these films demonstrate [. . .] It is nonetheless ironic that gay audiences should take such pleasure in films that so repeatedly celebrate heterosexual union and so consistently deny the existence of gay desire at all.[60]

Why exactly some gay men should feel an affiliation with – or take particular pleasure in – depictions of excess is open to debate. Male homosexuality has sometimes been understood or perceived as 'effeminate' behaviour, with gay men seen as more 'emotional' than heterosexual men. A gay male preference for melodramatic fictions, then, can be read as a pleasurable indulgence in such assumptions, whilst also contributing to their perpetuation. Alternatively, the link between excess and artifice may connect to gay men's understanding of role-playing, and 'life as theatre'. Queers grow up learning to disguise their sexual orientation in order to avoid prejudice and abuse, enabling recognition of how all identities – no matter how stable they seem – are fragile performances. For gay men (and other queers), the joy of melodrama may be its pervasive adoption of artifice and rejection of the codes of realism, implying the constructed nature of all personae. Finally, the excessive plots of melodrama may provide queer spectators with the sadistic pleasure of watching heterosexual characters suffer. Classical melodramas often portray characters who fail, quite spectacularly, to 'perform' their heterosexuality. The protagonists of *Stella Dallas* and *Mildred Pierce* (Curtiz, 1945) fail as mothers and lose their daughters (Stella's daughter leaves, Mildred's youngest dies). Families disintegrate in *Written on the Wind* and *Rebel Without a Cause*. Bette Davis in *Beyond the Forest* (Vidor, 1949) cannot fulfil her role as a wife and eventually perishes.

Connected to the concept of excess is camp. Historically, camp has been associated with gay male subcultures; Richard Dyer has defined it as 'a characteristically gay way of handling the values, images and products of the dominant culture through irony, exaggeration, trivialisation, theatricalisation and an ambivalent making fun of and out of the serious and respectable'.[61] However, since the 1960s – and, in particular, Susan Sontag's 1964 essay 'Notes on "Camp"', which brought the term to a much broader public – campness has been somewhat diffused, and taken up by mainstream culture.[62] Campness has maintained its currency within gay male culture, but what is sometimes known in contrast as 'mass camp' has spread elements of a camp approach beyond this demographic.

Classical Hollywood melodramas, of course, may have been consumed as camp at the time of their initial release by some audiences – the gay male pleasure in excess described above, for instance, can also be read as camp appreciation. However, as Barbara Klinger discusses, the consumption of classical melodramas by viewers in subsequent decades has often been through a 'mass camp' perspective which reads the films as outmoded and unintentionally comedic. As she writes,

Generally, film melodrama tends to emphasise the social mores of its time, as well as its styles and fashions. Hence, melodramas from the earliest days of cinema through the 1960s are liable to appear as keenly 'disempowered' in a contemporary context due to the sheer force of social change. Further, melodrama typically demonstrates an exaggerated dramatic logic and style that, through the passage of a few decades, can appear so in excess of contemporary realist norms that it attracts the camp penchant for the absurdly fantastic. In addition, some of melodrama's most definitive elements – its concentration on romance and male/female roles – are likely to register as camp, due to the effects of gender consciousness-raising through feminism and gay liberation. Through these kinds of historical incongruities, one decade's affecting emotional and visual experience serves to elicit a later period's parodic reflexes.[63]

Klinger goes on to isolate a range of aspects of Sirk's films (narrative conventions, lines of dialogue, and so on) that enable them to be read as camp; her arguments can also be applied to the retrospective consumption of many other classical melodramas.

It is worth pausing to note that *Far from Heaven*, despite featuring many of the excessive components previously described – stylised mise-en-scène and a non-realistic performance style, for instance – is not particularly camp. Many reviewers also noted this. Though the film may have caused some laughter in cinemas (as was identified earlier), the predominant response seems to have been of audiences experiencing emotional engagement. Ella Taylor, for instance, commented that '*Far from Heaven* is not a campy movie. True, it has its ironies, but though you can read it ironically if you wish, Haynes' triumph is that it also plays beautifully straight.'[64] The lack of campness may be due to the film's incorporation of elements that would not have been possible under the Hays Code, such as the romance between Cathy and Raymond. It might be related to the experience of watching contemporary actors in a historical setting, similar to that of watching other 'period dramas'. Or it could be the commitment of the filmmakers to the simulation, to producing a faithful homage rather than a parody.

Finally, and perhaps most problematically, the relationship between gay men and melodrama is often related to cross-gender spectator identification with female stars and characters. As Jane Shattuc has suggested, for example, 'Gays not only identified with the marginality of the melodramatic form as a "castrated culture", they displaced their sexual identities onto the melodrama's heroine as a victim of patriarchal discourses.'[65] Brett Farmer goes further than this, suggesting in his book *Spectacular Passions* that the bond of gay male spectators with female stars in melodrama is connected to the actresses' portrayal of mothers. Positioning his argument in relation to writings by John Fletcher, Leo Bersani and Kaja Silverman that valorise gay male matrocentric identification as rebellious and transgressive, he argues that 'gay audiences have long been drawn to the genre of Hollywood melodrama because it uniquely provides for a representation and exploration of the types of matrocentric scenarios central to gay male psychosexual paradigms.'[66] Certainly, gay male idolatry of female stars from the realms of cinema, television and music has a substantial history, and continues to endure. *Far from Heaven* even suggests, in its casting, that Julianne Moore may operate for some present-day gay viewers as a contemporary incarnation of Lana Turner or Jane Wyman.

The long-standing cultural association of gay men with the idolisation of certain classical Hollywood female stars, however, has been criticised in recent years. Daniel Harris, for instance, in *The Rise and Fall of Gay Culture*, sees such spectatorial relations as passé, an element of pre-Stonewall gay culture that has become unnecessary. In the wake of gay liberation, he asks, what value is there in gay viewers continuing to identify with (and weep along with) female victims of circumstance?[67] For Michael DeAngelis, the emphasis on gay men's relationship with female screen stars can prevent exploration and analysis of the bonds of attraction and identification that the same audience has with male stars.[68] Arriving in cinemas in the wake of such challenges, *Far from Heaven* not only invites audiences to consider how film genres have changed. It also says to contemporary gay male spectators, 'these are the kinds of characters and narratives that used to be of special significance to gay men' (and, of course, remain to some), and thus invites reflection on how their identificatory bonds with film stars and characters have altered.

Conclusion

Far from Heaven is the most formally generic of Todd Haynes's films to date; all of his others mix and match styles and genres. However, as this chapter has demonstrated, the film's adherence to a strict generic template enables it to provide a provocative exploration of the power and persistence of genre, and to enable reflection on the ways in which genres fade and mutate. In resuscitating a form of filmmaking associated with the 1950s, *Far from Heaven* invites contemporary audiences to recognise how significantly the form of the melodrama has altered in the last fifty years. For instance, contrasted with other films made in 2002 that could be described as 'family melodramas', *Far from Heaven* is almost unique in its intention to provoke tears from audiences. Indeed, one of the most important effects of the film is its invitation to audiences to consider how cinema induces emotional responses from viewers – and why crying at the cinema has become a rather rare experience. The last part of the discussion offered by this chapter began to open up the topic of the gay/queer significance of *Far from Heaven*. The next (and final) chapter examines this subject in more substantial detail and scope.

4. Queerness

Throughout the previous chapters of this book, weaving through the explorations of independent cinema, authorship and the genre of melodrama, the subject of homosexuality and queerness has repeatedly surfaced. Observations have been made relating to the politics of sexuality in the film, challenges to cinema authorship made by queer directors, and so on. Due to the inclusion of Frank's narrative thread in *Far from Heaven*, and Todd Haynes's insights regarding the ways in which his sexual orientation influences his filmmaking, it would have been perverse not to devote some space to this topic. And yet, there is a great deal more to be said regarding the queerness of *Far from Heaven*. (Indeed, for many viewers of Haynes's film, the very experience of watching a Sirkian melodrama on the big screen in the first years of the twenty-first century may have seemed rather queer.) For all of its apparent conventionality – strict adherence to a generic template, linear narrative, classical score, and so on – *Far from Heaven* is also a deeply political film. As has been explored already, this is in part related to the resuscitation of an outmoded melodramatic mode, and to the incorporation into that form of 1950s understandings of sexuality and race mostly absent from classical instances of the genre. But the political significance of the film extends beyond this – and, I want to argue, in ways that are evidently 'queer', affected by and related to queer activism, criticism and film practice.

This chapter, then, introduces the term 'queer', the history of queer politics and praxis, and the field of critical enquiry known as queer theory, and explores ways in which insights and arguments from this arena can be used to analyse and understand *Far from Heaven*. In particular, I will be suggesting that the film's queerness can be identified in four specific ways. Firstly, in its bringing to mainstream audiences an 'independent', 'art-house' or 'underground' attitude and approach to melodrama; secondly, in the supporting characters of Sybil (Viola Davis), Eleanor (Patricia Clarkson) and Mona (Celia Weston); thirdly, in its impact on contemporary audiences' understandings and readings of cinema history; and fourthly, in its relation to HIV/AIDS and public responses to the disease.

'Queer', Queer Politics and Queer Theory

Prior to the late 1980s, the word 'queer' was almost always utilised as a term of abuse, directed against those seen as sexual 'others' in order to mark their (inferior) difference from the heterosexual mainstream. The 1980s and 1990s, however, saw an appropriation and reclamation of the term by some of those who had been stigmatised by its use.[1] That is, members of a disenfranchised group took up a pejorative label used against them, revelled in it and attempted, as Richard Dyer notes,

not so much to cleanse it of its negative associations as to challenge the assumption that those associations are in fact negative – thus immorality may be a challenge to repressive morality, deviance a rejection of the straight and thus narrow, and what is considered sordid and disgusting may in fact be exciting, risky, a life lived to the full on the edge.[2]

The reclamation of the word 'queer' was widespread, and needs to be understood in relation to the historical and cultural context of the time.

By the late 1980s, there was a prevalent and pervasive dissatisfaction with the repressive politics, attitudes, morality and policies instituted and nurtured by the dominant Conservative and Republican parties in, respectively, the United Kingdom and United States. This discontent and frustration was experienced by many people across Britain and the United States, but was especially marked for those whose opportunities to live as equal citizens had been restricted or proscribed. On the whole, the atmosphere of the decade had been one that was largely reactionary and stifling; many of the gains of the anti-war groups and civil rights movements of the 1960s and 1970s had been lost, retracted, outlawed or overruled, in favour of a socially conformist, morally stifling society which decried (and often persecuted) dissent. For lesbians and gay men, the 1980s were an especially difficult time. Many legal inequalities identified and targeted by the gay rights movement had not been overturned. Homophobia was rife and often institutionally sanctioned. Perhaps most importantly, the spread of HIV/AIDS in both Britain and the United States was initially largely ignored by the dominant political parties. Something of a crisis point was reached at the end of the 1980s, coincidentally also the time when Margaret Thatcher was re-elected for a third term of government, and Ronald Reagan was replaced in the White House by the equally right-wing George Bush. A large number of lesbian and gay individuals (and others also feeling the strain) believed that something had to be done to break the forceful imposition of these oppressive political systems; the expression of dissent, irrespective of form or consequences, had become a fundamental necessity. Broadly speaking, then, the reclamation of the term 'queer' can be seen to mark the 'moment' of this dissatisfaction and the concomitant desire to revolt.

One marked result of this dissatisfaction was the formation of a number of new political collectives conducting a range of activist activities, and using 'queer' as a form of self-nomination in their rhetoric and publicity. These include the US groups Queer Nation and ACT-UP; as noted in Chapter 2, Todd Haynes was affiliated with the latter. Prior to the inauguration of a specifically 'queer' politics, there had, of course, been a range of attempts at political organisation and demonstration by groups whose constituent members affiliated together on the grounds of their shared sexual identity. The most notable precursor is the gay rights movement, which took shape around, and became significantly visible in the immediate aftermath of, the New York Stonewall riots of June 1969. But the gay rights movement of the 1970s – with its annual Pride parades, 'Gay is Good' sloganeering, and assimilationist aims – was, internally, a politically troubled one. Many lesbians, for instance, often felt alienated, even ostracised, from politics, actions and interests they believed were largely dictated by gay men; the gay rights movement was also predominantly run by and for white, middle-class individuals. This led to splits, divisions and factionalism. In contrast, queer political organisations attempted to overcome these differences. By the late 1980s, the experience of oppression was so heavily marked for so many different people that the need for coalitions between those formerly at loggerheads became of paramount importance. In addition, a large number of lesbians, gay men and sexual 'others' believed that the assimilationist policies of the gay rights activists of the 1970s and 1980s had been, on the whole, unsuccessful – and that more radical strategies were necessary. These new 'queer' groups did not replace older lesbian and gay organisations, many of which continued to operate.

One issue which separates lesbian and gay activism from queer

organisations is a differing approach to understanding identity categories. Where lesbian and gay politics are normally grounded in essentialist beliefs, the birth of queer activism incorporated the recognition
that individual identity labels – 'black', 'woman', 'lesbian' – are always
insufficient to capture the messiness of any one individual's complex
identity, an identity which, moreover, may be susceptible to change
over time. In addition, admission was made that particular terms only
make sense within individual countries or cultures, during specific eras.
Acknowledgement of the cultural and historical contingency of identity
labels, and their insufficiency *as* labels, entailed a suspicion regarding the
use of relatively stable terms such as 'lesbian and gay'. As Eve Sedgwick
wrote in *Tendencies*, a key queer theory text,

one of the things that 'queer' can refer to [is] the open mesh of possibilities, gaps,
overlaps, dissonances and resonances, lapses and excesses of meaning when the
constituent elements of anyone's gender, of anyone's sexuality aren't made (or
can't be made) to signify monolithically.[3]

Or, as Donald Hall has suggested, 'queer' 'is to abrade the classifications,
to sit athwart conventional categories or traverse several'.[4]

Temporally lagging slightly behind the advent of queer politics and
activism, queer theory emerged as a 'new' field of academic endeavour
in the early 1990s. This was roughly coterminous with the appearance
of New Queer Cinema, the film movement with which Haynes has been
associated. The first appearance of the phrase 'queer theory' is usually
attributed to Teresa de Lauretis, the editor of an issue of the feminist
journal *differences* in 1991 devoted to 'Queer Theory: Lesbian and Gay
Sexualities'; the articles in this journal issue covered a range of disparate topics, including lesbian fetishism and gay male narrative practice.
Swiftly after the appearance of this volume, queer theory proliferated: a
number of conferences took place, 'special' issues of journals appeared,
and a variety of books were published.[5] Although this wealth of material
has covered (and continues to cover) a diffuse range of subjects, Tamsin
Spargo offers a useful summary of the field:

Queer theory is not a singular or systematic conceptual or methodological
framework, but a collection of intellectual engagements with the relations
between sex, gender and sexual desire. If queer theory is a school of thought,
then it's one with a highly unorthodox view of discipline. The term describes a
diverse range of critical practices and priorities: readings of the representation

of same-sex desire in literary texts, films, music, images; analyses of the social and political power relations of sexuality; critiques of the sex-gender system; studies of transsexual and transgender identification, of sadomasochism and of transgressive desires.[6]

Bringing these strands together, it can be asserted that the field is, almost always, concerned in some way with understandings of (non-normative, contra-heterosexual) identity. Since Spargo attempted her summary in 1999, queer theory has continued to mutate and develop. In addition to continued explorations of the subjects mentioned by Spargo, queer theory has recently examined topics including time and temporality, and shame and negative feeling. The journal *GLQ* serves as a valuable index of the issues and subjects considered at the forefront of the field.

Perhaps the major difference between 'lesbian and gay' theory and activism, and that gathered under the 'queer' rubric, is that the former mostly works with an essentialist understanding of identity, whilst the latter frequently troubles the stability of identity categories, repeatedly flagging up their limitations. The pervasive adoption of this model of understanding identity throughout queer theory can, arguably, be traced to the writings of two key authors whose opinions and ideas are central to the field: Michel Foucault and Judith Butler. Foucault's *The History of Sexuality, Volume 1: The Will to Knowledge* (1976) and Butler's *Gender Trouble* (1990) and *Bodies that Matter* (1993) all posited radical understandings of sexuality and challenges to historical understandings of identity categories that have continued to reverberate through and influence subsequent queer theoretical writings.[7]

Although providing an overview of the entire realm of queer theory is beyond the scope of this book, it is worth highlighting the variety of work that has been produced by queer film theorists and the sorts of insights that they have offered. Queer theoretical writings on film are indebted to the work of several pioneer cinema critics and academics, including Richard Dyer, Vito Russo, Parker Tyler, Andrea Weiss and Robin Wood.[8] Indeed, specific instances of queer film theory can be identified as developments from, or against, particular writings by these authors. (Russo's *The Celluloid Closet*, an evaluative history of homosexuality in the movies first published in 1981, is both a foundational text, and regularly challenged by queer film theorists for the judgements and proclamations it contains.) There are particular topics which recur throughout the queer film theory realm; these include retrospective readings, stars and stardom, and spectatorship. It is worth providing a brief introduction to each of these subjects, in order to convey a flavour of the field.

Firstly, a notable strand of queer film theory is concerned with the retroactive 'discovery' or uncovering of 'queer' impulses within a range of particular cinematic texts – that is, with the queering of film history. Most often, these movies are canonical 'classics' of Hollywood origin. For example, Alexander Doty and Robert Lang, separately, have provided queer historical readings of a broad range of (mostly mainstream American) films, from *The Wizard of Oz* (Fleming, 1939) to *Citizen Kane* (Welles, 1941).[9] The desire to identify a queer presence within, and to enable queer viewing pleasure in consuming, this variety of films can be seen to relate to the queer activist drive to occupy, transform and pervert spaces of geography and representation which have ignored or excluded the non-normative. In addition, it demonstrates a willingness to undertake what Jennifer Terry has termed 'deviant historiography': that is, to proffer alternative accounts of history, whilst also, by projecting queerness backwards, troubling the notion of a concrete, temporally linear, logically unfurling history.[10] I will be reading *Far from Heaven* as a clear model of queer rereading later in this chapter.

A second crucial focus for queer film theorists is the 'queerness' of specific stars. Analyses on this topic mostly provide assessments of the star images of particular actors and actresses around whom there is queer interest: in other words, individuals who are regularly cast in queer character roles, who incorporate a certain queer ambiguity into their star personae, or who accrue a variety of queer fans. Pee Wee Herman/Paul Reubens, James Dean, Mel Gibson, Keanu Reeves and Jodie Foster are among those stars whose queerness has been subject to queer theoretical exploration.[11] As with the retroactive readings, on the whole, such accounts strive to identify and articulate queer positions within, or in relation to, mainstream cinema and its history. I will explore the queerness of specific actors and narrative positions shortly.

Thirdly, queer spectatorship is a major concern for queer film theory. 'Classic' film theoretical accounts of cinema viewing – mainly deriving from, and rooted in, Laura Mulvey's foundational essay of 1975, 'Visual Pleasure and Narrative Cinema' – have had little place for the lesbian, gay, bisexual or queer spectator.[12] And yet, evidently, queers are a substantial presence in many cinema audiences. (Indeed, Brett Farmer has argued that gay men have a 'special relationship' to cinema.[13]) Some queer film theorists, then, have attempted to address whether classical spectatorship paradigms can accommodate, or be reconstructed to account for, queer subjects and their viewing pleasures.[14] Other authors have claimed that such endeavours rest on rather naïve essentialist assumptions, and that a more deconstructively 'queer' understanding of spectatorship is possible. Thus, Judith Mayne has asserted that:

> Film theory has been so bound by the heterosexual symmetry that supposedly governs Hollywood cinema that it has ignored the possibility, for instance, that one of the distinct pleasures of the cinema may well be a 'safe zone' in which homosexual as well as heterosexual desires can be fantasised and acted out. I am not speaking here of an innate capacity to 'read against the grain', but rather of the way in which desire and pleasure in the cinema may well function to problematize the categories of heterosexual versus homosexual.[15]

It is possible, of course, to adopt both positions. Brett Farmer, for instance, has proposed a model of queer spectatorship which sits somewhere between essentialist and post-structuralist accounts of identity – an understanding that recognises the problems with both conceptions of subjectivity and agency.[16]

In addition to these three topics, queer film theorists have explored a wide range of additional themes and concerns. However, as with the rest of this introductory section of the chapter, my intention has been merely to plot and roughly sketch the roots of queer politics and theory, to highlight connections between the two, and to proffer some examples of queer approaches to culture and representation. In the following four sections, more sustained queer analyses of particular topics will be presented, enabling an understanding of the potential impact and insight available through adopting a queer theoretical paradigm.

Queering Melodrama

The first queer strategy that can be employed to configure *Far from Heaven* queerly relates to the film's generic status as a melodrama. In Chapter 1, Haynes's film was identified as occupying a position partway between the independent and mainstream sectors; although the project began life outside of the studios, it received financial support and distribution from what became the specialty division of Universal. Chapter 2 acknowledged the long list of films and directors directly referenced or alluded to in *Far from Heaven*, from *All That Heaven Allows* to *The Reckless Moment*, from several films by Otto Preminger to Hitchcock's

Marnie. Almost all of the films listed, aside from Fassbinder's *Angst essen Seele auf/Fear Eats the Soul*, were mainstream titles produced and distributed from within the Hollywood studio system. And yet there has also been a parallel history of melodrama production, by gay men, that has operated either independent of the studios or in an art-house context. In these films, a gay or queer sensibility is clearly in operation, inflecting aspects from set design to performance style, dialogue to narrative, and effectively perverting the standardised form of the genre. *Far from Heaven* also needs to be positioned in relation to this alternative history; made by a gay man with a history of working in low-budget queer cinema, and only partly financed by a major entertainment conglomerate's specialty label, Haynes's film arguably has more in common with these non-mainstream titles and needs to be seen as a key text in this lineage. Indeed, I want to argue here that Haynes has taken elements and tactics from some of these gay/queer alternative and art-house films, and introduced them into his 'Indiewood' production, blurring further the distinction between the mainstream and its others. In so doing, he succeeded in bringing those different perspectives to the multiplex, expanding the size and form of the audience paying to view a queer take on the melodrama beyond subcultural denizens and the art-house elite.

Before identifying the aspects of this parallel field of production that Haynes employed in the production of *Far from Heaven*, it is worth sketching out a brief history of gay/queer alternative and art-house melodrama production. As was discussed in Chapter 3, homosexuality operated as a subtext or coded erotic charge within key examples of Hollywood melodrama of the 1950s, from *Rebel Without a Cause* to *Suddenly, Last Summer*. Around the same time, underground gay directors started to pay homage to (and parody the excesses of) these mainstream efforts, inaugurating a lineage of fringe-operation queer cinema that has persisted to date. Twin filmmakers George and Mike Kuchar have both regularly plundered from mainstream melodrama in their output. Working together in the 1950s and early 1960s, their films had lascivious and provocative titles that often cheekily referenced mainstream works: *The Naked and the Nude* (1957), *Pussy on a Hot Tin Roof* (1961), *Born of the Wind* (1961), *The Lovers of Eternity* (1963). George Kuchar's solo output, more than that of his brother, has continued to reference mainstream melodrama in projects such as *Hold Me While I'm Naked* (1966), *Color Me Shameless* (1967) and *A Reason to Live* (1976).

At the same time as the Kuchar brothers were starting their careers in cinema, other New York-based gay men were referencing melodrama in their own low-budget films. Jack Smith made few films in his lifetime; he remains best known for *Flaming Creatures* (1963), which caused some controversy due to its sexual content. Smith was entranced by a history of ignored stars and generic mainstream cinema – he paid tribute to Maria Montez, star of forgotten B-pictures such as *Cobra Woman* (Siodmak, 1944), in an essay published in *Film Culture* magazine in the early 1960s.[17] Andy Warhol, in contrast to Smith, made hundreds of films (if one includes all of his three-minute 'screen tests'). Though many of his earlier movies can be seen as experiments with duration, stock and documentary form, later semi-scripted efforts – such as *Kitchen* or *Poor Little Rich Girl* (both 1965, both written by Ronald Tavel) – reference melodrama in their emphasis on domestic spaces, ennui and mundane conversations about relationships. The same tone is also used, in a more conventionally narrative format, by Paul Morrissey in his trilogy of Warhol-produced films starring Joe Dallesandro, *Flesh* (1968), *Trash* (1970) and *Heat* (1972). Jim Bidgood's *Pink Narcissus* (1971), though essentially free of narrative, depicts protagonist Bobby Kendall within artificial environments saturated with lurid colours and excessive props, accompanied by a lush orchestral score and torchsongs. Although it was shot in Bidgood's apartment, the opulent sets and their striking colour schemes recall the films of Sirk.

In Europe, three gay male directors are noteworthy for their appropriation of the melodrama in their own work: Rainer Werner Fassbinder, Pedro Almodóvar and François Ozon. Fassbinder has already been mentioned. A key figure within the New German Cinema of the 1970s, he was a prolific filmmaker who produced forty feature films during his short career. (He died at the age of 37.) His early works were experimental and avant-garde, but he directed a series of films in the early 1970s – including *The Merchant of Four Seasons* (1972), *The Bitter Tears of Petra von Kant* (1972), *Fear Eats the Soul* and *Fox and his Friends* (1975) – which were all indebted to American melodrama, especially the films of Sirk. Fassbinder's films were often critical of the German bourgeoisie, and he identified in Sirk's 1950s films for Ross Hunter how a generic cinema form could be employed to provide political critique. Almodóvar's earlier films, such as *Labyrinth of Passion* (1982) and *What Have I Done To Deserve This?* (1984), were often anarchic and designed to shock. Beginning with *Women on the Verge of a Nervous Breakdown* (1988), however, his films have regularly been constructed as melodramas, centred on female protagonists, with romantic entanglements and family-related incidents and escapades providing the main material for the plots. *High Heels* (1991), *The Flower of My Secret* (1995), *All About My Mother* (1999), *Volver* (2006) and others can all be seen as takes on melodrama in a contemporary Spanish setting, with Almodóvar adding a queer register to each film. This tone is produced despite the fact that Almodóvar's protagonists are usually heterosexual, through the use of such elements as strong primary colours, sparky dialogue, and an evocative and emotive use of Spanish popular music. Further, as Mercer and Shingler note,

> The gay sensibility in his films is expressed through narrative twists and turns that confound our conventional expectations of heterosexual romance, the inclusion of characters whose sexuality is ambiguous or whose sexual identity or gender identities are in flux [. . .] The recurrence of these characters creates a sense of a world in which preconceptions of 'normal' sexual behaviour are constantly questioned and undermined.[18]

François Ozon's relationship to melodrama is less pronounced than those of Fassbinder and Almodóvar. Across his productive career, his films have mostly adopted an 'art cinema' form, with occasional experimentation with generic form. Two specific titles are worthy of note. *Water Drops on Burning Rocks* (2000) was adapted from a Fassbinder play, and features lead characters with notably fluid sexual orientations. In contrast, *8 Women* (2002) is a drawing-room murder mystery with musical numbers that is blatantly influenced by classical Hollywood cinema. The film's most obvious reference is *The Women* (Cukor, 1939), although there are also fleeting allusions to Rita Hayworth's dance routine in *Gilda* (Vidor, 1946), to the deer in the snow in *All That Heaven Allows*, and to the opening credits sequence of *Imitation of Life*.

There are numerous additional examples of gay/queer underground and alternative pastiches and appropriations of the melodrama. Several films by John Waters are evidently indebted to the genre: *The Diane Linkletter Story* (1970), *Female Trouble* (1974), and most notably *Polyester* (1981). In the latter, Divine plays suburban housewife Francine Fishpaw, who has an unfaithful husband, a stroppy, slutty daughter and a delinquent, glue-sniffing son. Sinking into depression and despair, Francine meets Todd Tomorrow (Tab Hunter) and romance blossoms. But Todd turns out to be having an affair with Francine's mother La Rue, with the pair planning to embezzle Francine's money. A similarly hyperbolic narrative is to be found in the gaudily designed New Zealand period drama *Desperate Remedies* (Main/Wells, 1992), which features complex sexual and romantic connections between the characters, including a lesbian relationship. On a much lower budget, Bruce LaBruce's black and white *No Skin Off My Ass* (1991) reworks Robert Altman's (already perverse) melodrama *That Cold Day in the Park* (1969) to focus on a gay relationship between a hairdresser and a skinhead, including graphic depictions of sex between the pair.

In all of the examples mentioned, the gay/queer male directors working outside of the mainstream adopt, borrow from and play with melodrama as a generic form. At times, the excess and hyperbole associated with the genre are pushed to extremes, as in *Polyester*. Narrative form may be fairly faithfully maintained, as with Ozon's *8 Women*, or deconstructed into fragments, as George Kuchar does in *A Reason to Live*. A crucial question to raise is why so many gay male filmmakers have been driven to construct their own homages or perversions of melodrama. As was identified in Chapter 3, there has been a long-standing relationship and association between gay men and melodrama, arguably equal only to that between the same demographic and the musical. With gay characters almost entirely absent from the narratives of mainstream classical melodramas, though, these underground, alternative and art-house films can be understood as attempts at rectification, and at making overt the queer appeal of the genre. Mercer and Shingler propose additional reasons for the existence of this separate lineage of production, identifying 'camp' as one key explanation, as:

> melodramatic, 'over the top' narratives and stylistic techniques draw attention in a parodic sense to the artificial construction of gender roles and the norms of heterosexual romance. Another explanation might be that openly gay filmmakers entering the mainstream of culture have to use a recognisable, if anachronistic, rhetoric to situate gay desire because wider heterosexual culture has neither a visual or emotional language to adequately articulate gay desire, existing as it still does outside of societal norms.[19]

Certainly, just as many classical melodramas (including those of Sirk) can now be appreciated through a camp lens, so the dominant tone of many of the films named here is campy parody, though with a particularly queer emphasis on deconstructive excess. Further, gay/queer directors have also borrowed from other mainstream generic forms – horror, the musical, the period drama – in a similar manner, highlighting and making up for the omissions in the classical instances of each genre, often through pastiche or substantial fragmentation and appropriation, and in order to experiment with and rework recognised narrative formats.

That Haynes has taken substantial elements from classical mainstream movies in *Far from Heaven* is evident. However, his film is also indebted to the lineage of underground and art-house production outlined above. As was noted in Chapter 1, Haynes wanted to take the adoption of Sirkian style beyond anything that director achieved, which has the effect of pushing particular sequences close to parodic excess. This can be seen in such scenes as the blue-and-purple-lit interaction following the Whitakers' party in which Cathy and Frank fail to have sex, and she almost shouts 'You're all men to me, Frank, and *all man!*' to a rising dramatic score. Or, indeed, that in which the Whitaker family exchange their Christmas presents in front of the fire, the artifice and gaudiness of the décor, props and costume design notably amplified; Cathy's dress design, for instance, is located somewhere between busy wrapping paper and a decorated Christmas tree. Here, *Far from Heaven*'s visual aesthetic is not too distant from the patent fakeness of *Pink Narcissus*. An additional element of *Far from Heaven*'s distinctive style is the performance mode of the cast; as identified in Chapter 1, this is notably different from regular mainstream codes of realism. This performance style – arch, mannered, indebted to historical forms of screen acting – can be compared with that adopted in films by the Kuchar brothers, Andy Warhol and John Waters. Although there are observable differences in the acting styles utilised in the movies by these directors (the cartoonish characters in *Polyester*, for instance, exclaim many of their lines), all experiment with vocal flatness, volume and timbre, and dialogue delivery in ways that set their work apart from the conventional.

A number of critics and theorists have noted that *Far from Heaven* introduces homosexuality into the form of the classical melodrama, which has the effect of commenting on the closeted identity of stars such as Rock Hudson, the narrative evasions of the films based on Tennessee Williams plays, and so on.[20] However, earlier instances of independent, experimental or art-house queer melodrama featured overtly gay/queer characters. Fassbinder's *The Bitter Tears of Petra von Kant* focuses on a lesbian couple, while *Fox and his Friends* exposes and dissects class-based prejudice amongst a group of gay men. LaBruce's take on Altman shifts narrative focus from a heterosexual couple to a queer one. In

Almodóvar's *All About My Mother*, one of the key characters, Agrado, is transsexual. Finally, Haynes's blatant borrowing or theft from mainstream movies – *All That Heaven Allows*, *The Reckless Moment* – is also a tactic employed by Ozon in *8 Women* and LaBruce in *No Skin Off My Ass*.

All of these techniques and tactics – hyperbolic mise-en-scène, a performance style distinct from contemporary realist conventions, the explicit incorporation of gay and queer characters into a genre from which they have mostly been historically absent, blatant borrowings from other films – were identified in earlier discussions as facets of *Far from Heaven* that can mark it as 'independent'. Viewing the film through a queer optic, however, and positioning it as belonging to a lineage of experimental and art-house films by gay male directors which pay homage to or appropriate the melodrama, enables a recognition that Haynes's use and combination of these elements is a concerted attempt to contribute to the tradition, and to bring queer melodrama to a wider audience.

The Queerness of Secondary Characters

A second approach to *Far from Heaven* that enables recognition of its queerness relates to the casting and characterisation of its secondary or supporting characters. Again, at first glance, and in keeping with the film's strict adherence to a generic template, the supporting characters may not seem markedly different from those in other mainstream films. However, a number of queer writers and theorists (including Michael Bronski, Judith Roof and Patricia White, all discussed below) have explored the significance of the role of the supporting character, and *Far from Heaven* serves as a model example of the subversive potential this element of a film can carry. Here, I will concentrate on three particular characters: Cathy's best friend, Eleanor Fine (Patricia Clarkson); town gossip, Mona Lauder (Celia Weston); and the Whitakers' maid, Sybil (Viola Davis).

While the main plot of *Far from Heaven* features a narrative thread concerned with homosexuality, this is a fairly conventional tale of a husband coming to terms with his sexuality and leaving his wife. The more queer moments in the narrative – queer in the sense of being surprising, disruptive, unexpected, unconventional – are associated with the secondary characters. Operating on the periphery, they are more knowledgeable, sassy and perceptive than the leads. Mona and Eleanor are much more sussed about homosexuality than Cathy, with Mona accompanying a gay man to the art opening at which Cathy and Raymond discuss Miró; Eleanor coerces her female pals into a conversation about sex, and has the bawdiest anecdote; both Mona and Sybil, astute readers of the subtleties of social interaction, correctly identify Cathy and Raymond's romantic interest in each other whilst watching from the sidelines. In this, they perpetuate a tradition of supporting characters with particular appeal to queer audiences.

Michael Bronski, in his book *Culture Clash*, identifies the appeal of some supporting characters – and the actresses who play them – for gay men:

the sidekick's role was generally to act as a confidante and to give the audience a pungent analysis of the plot. Sidekicks were sarcastic, unromantic, and sensible. They were cleverly self-deprecating . . . but could also turn the wit on men. Too smart ever to get the man, sidekicks had to settle for being funnier than everybody else. For gay men who would never walk off into the sunset with a leading man, the sidekick was a dose of real life.[21]

Crucially, the supporting character is also often coded as 'queer' – or, at the very least, not written and played as clearly heterosexual. In a consideration of secondary characters and their relationship to narrative structure, Judith Roof argues that the middle of a film – the second act of three – is a space of 'uncertainty, chaos, and misdirection', and the narrative time associated with secondary characters. As she writes,

Main characters may triumph (or fail) at film's end, but female comic secondary characters play in the middle, producing and sorting confusions and anxieties, threatening short circuits of narrative, and helping the narrative along. They provide humour, wisdom, a point of identification, and the possibility of narrative alternatives until they disappear at the end. They are the site where minor, middle, and perverse overlap, undoing narrative as they do it and showing us another way to look.[22]

This perversity has also been noted by Patricia White, in an essay on Agnes Moorehead: 'At once essential to classical realism and marginal to its narrative goals, the supporting character is a site for the encoding of the threat and the promise of female deviance.'[23] As she goes on to observe, 'Nurses, secretaries, career women, nuns, companions, and housekeepers connote, not lesbian identity, but a deviation from heterosexualised femininity.'[24]

Although Eleanor Fine does not fit into one of these roles – she is the 'homemaker' wife of Stan Fine (Michael Gaston), who works at Magnatech with Frank Whitaker – she is the most fully fleshed-out supporting character in *Far from Heaven*. The role of Eleanor contributes substantially to *Far from Heaven*'s particular queer register. In significant part this is due to the casting of Patricia Clarkson in the role. Like many supporting actors, she tends to play characters whose sexuality is ambiguous, incomplete, uncategorisable – or largely irrelevant to her plot arc, which may leave that aspect of her role unexplored. As identified in Chapter 1, despite parts in a number of mainstream films, Clarkson is an actress largely associated with the independent film sector. Well-received roles as a has-been German actress strung out on heroin in *High Art*, and as Sarah O'Connor, the artist younger sister of repressed matriarch Ruth Fisher in the HBO TV series *Six Feet Under*, have contributed to her status as a character actress known for an angular physicality, distinctively husky voice, and ability to emote with skill. The voice is significant here: an argument could be made that one aspect that sets the supporting character apart from the leads, and that codes him or her as 'different', is their voice (notably deep, high, harsh, soft or accented). As Clarkson has said,

I was somewhat typecast as suburban 'mom' type roles early on. But I've always had this deep voice, so I think it was tough for directors to cast me as the ingénue. Because I'd walk in and look a certain way, then open my mouth and have this . . . voice![25]

Clarkson's personal life is kept largely out of the press, which allows viewer understandings of her star image to prioritise her film and television roles over her romantic entanglements. She has been linked with actor Campbell Scott but, in an interview with Michael Musto in *The Village Voice*, made the rather queer claim that:

I've never wanted to be married, and I knew it at 14. I knew I wouldn't have this life if I got married. I've had beautiful relationships with men, and I hope to continue to do so till I'm 100, but I could never live a conventional life. I'm claustrophobic. I can't do a TV series, and I can't get married. I can't do one thing for a long time!

Contributing further to an understanding of Clarkson as unconventional and liberal, she gave a speech in support of gay rights entitled 'Here's to the Violets' at a Human Rights Campaign rally in New Orleans in 2009.

In *Far from Heaven*, Eleanor's role as Cathy's best friend is complex: she defends and supports Cathy, but her political attitudes are muddy. After Frank bruises Cathy's forehead, Eleanor notices and probes, but Cathy is unable to talk about her marital problems. When Cathy later confesses Frank's gayness to Eleanor, the latter is supportive, but iterates the belief that homosexuality should be kept separate from the impressionable and vulnerable: 'Oh you dear, sweet kid. In a million years I couldn't have imagined. *Not Frank!* I suppose divorce really is the only option – if only to keep it as far from the children as possible.' Eleanor also defends Cathy against allegations, made by Mona, that she is having an affair with Raymond. When Eleanor is subsequently made aware of Cathy's feelings for Raymond, she physically and emotionally turns away from her friend. Cathy denies that anything occurred with Raymond – and aside from the slow dance at the bar, nothing did happen. But Eleanor is hurt: 'Cathy, it's none of my business. But you certainly make it sound as if something did.' It is unclear whether this personal slight is caused simply by Cathy's clandestine emotions, now brought to light, or whether it also relates specifically to Cathy's involvement with a black man. Eleanor, after all, is one of the two people who ribs Cathy for the *Hartford Weekly Gazette* article which claims that Cathy is 'as devoted to her family as she is kind to Negroes' (the other is Dick Dawson, at the Whitakers' party).

Eleanor may not approve of 'liberal causes' – at the least, she finds them worthy of mockery. However, she is also the most knowledgeable character in *Far from Heaven* when it comes to the topic of homosexuality, and has the linguistic skill and terminology to discuss the subject. This is made clear in an exchange with Cathy about the upcoming art show opening, as Cathy is leaving Eleanor's home:

Eleanor: 'I'm sorry to say Mona Lauder *will* be attending. Turns out her uncle's in town, some hotshot art dealer from New York. I think I met him at one of Mona's soirées. A bit flowery for my taste.'
Cathy: 'How do you mean?'
Eleanor: 'Oh, you know. A touch light on his feet.'
Cathy: 'You mean . . .'
Eleanor: 'Yes, darling. One of *those*. Of course, I could be mistaken. Just an impression I got.'
Cathy: 'You don't care for them particularly?'
Eleanor: 'Well no, not particularly. Not that I actually *know* any.'

When Cathy seems to be taking a particular interest in this subject, Eleanor questions her investment:

Cathy: 'I read an article recently. In a magazine. [She closes the car door]. *What?*'

Eleanor: '*Nothing!* I'm just delighted to see you taking interest in yet another civic cause! I can see it now: "Cathleen Whitaker and her kindness to homosexuals"!'

Cathy: 'Oh – that word.'

This is an important exchange, for a number of reasons. Firstly, it demonstrates Eleanor's knowledge of euphemisms used to refer to homosexuality, as well as her ability to use the correct word directly. This is in stark contrast to Frank and Cathy's stumbling exchanges about the subject, and to Frank's psychiatrist, who only refers to homosexuality as 'this *sort* of behaviour' before clinically describing potential courses of treatment. Secondly, Eleanor displays relatively competent 'gaydar': she is able to identify Mona's uncle correctly as a homosexual. (This being said, she fails to spot Frank's closeted identity.) Thirdly, along with her other jokes at Cathy's expense, this exchange clearly positions Eleanor as the film's comic foil. Though her 'gags' are often rooted in one-upmanship, mild social prejudice or caustic commentary on the foibles of her friends, Eleanor at least entertains – her social group and the film's audience – through attempts at comedy. Cathy, in contrast, never cracks a joke; she probably could not.

Mona Lauder is a minor presence in *Far from Heaven* compared to Eleanor, but leaves her mark. She appears at the art opening with Morris Farnsworth, the gay uncle. While Cathy is chatting with Raymond about painting and spirituality, their conversation is briefly interrupted by noise from Mona, Morris and two other women, who are clearly gossiping about Cathy's social interaction with a black man. Later, as Cathy and Raymond arrive at Ernie's bar, Mona is picking up her vehicle from a car wash opposite; climbing into the driver's seat, she spots Cathy and Raymond, pauses, and smirks (see Figure 9). Although she is not seen again on screen, Mona subsequently wrecks havoc, spreading rumours about Cathy and Raymond's relationship – and thus operating as Judith Roof's typical destructive secondary character, 'producing . . . confusions and anxieties'. Mona Lauder – her name carefully constructed, it would seem, to suggest both 'moaning'

Figure 9 Mona Lauder spots Cathy and Raymond (© Focus Features/Vulcan Productions)

and 'louder', whilst also referencing the character of Mona Plash (Jacqueline de Wit) in *All That Heaven Allows* – is responsible through her loose tongue for Cathy being shunned at her daughter's ballet recital, for a domestic argument between Frank and Cathy ('the whole friggin' town's been talking!', he yells), and ultimately for Cathy's recognition that she has to fire Raymond and never see him again. Her gossip is also the root cause of Raymond's daughter Sarah being chased and attacked by three schoolboys – as one of them says to Sarah, 'Where do you think you're going? Home to see your daddy? Yeah, and his white girlfriend?'

Given the damage she causes, queer spectators may not want to claim Mona as a productive political figure. However, she is an identifiably perverse character: not paired off with a boyfriend or husband, friend of a fruity relation, overt and unabashed gossip, and wrecker of heterosexual relationships (whether or not those cross racial lines). The casting of Celia Weston contributes to her 'otherness'. Weston is a recognisable character actress – she is tall, not conventionally beautiful and rather thick-set. Born in Spartanburg, North Carolina, she often plays mothers from the Southern States, her 'Deep South' accent a recognisable connection between many of her roles. Her large size, bright mane, rich voice and tendency to wear gaudy make-up (bright blue eye-shadow, crimson lipstick) can give her the appearance of a transvestite or drag queen. Mona's destructive impulses may actually align her more obviously with queer politics than Eleanor – operating on the periphery,

Figure 10 Sybil watches Cathy and Raymond (© Focus Features/Vulcan Productions)

cut out from the regulated heterosexual economy of Hartford, Mona smashes all she can with the power of her words.

Sybil is an altogether different figure, but fits Patricia White's category of the 'housekeeper' secondary character. Named after the maid in *The Reckless Moment*, Sybil operates in a similar manner to that character; although she speaks very little and remains deferential to her employer throughout *Far from Heaven*, she is often placed in a position of knowledge. Sybil watches the development of the relationship between Cathy and Raymond, without offering comment or advice, just as the maid in *The Reckless Moment* has some silent awareness of Lucia Harper's blackmail problems. Indeed, at key moments Sybil is depicted looking through windows, watching the interactions of Cathy and Raymond (see Figure 10). Although she initially keeps the information from Cathy, Sybil knows that it was Raymond's daughter who was injured by the group of boys. When Cathy finds out, Sybil is able to tell Cathy Raymond's address and offers to accompany Cathy, with the implication being that a white woman should perhaps not travel alone into a black neighbourhood. This relationship between servants or maids and knowledge often appears in melodrama. As Finch and Kwietniowski write, in relation to *Maurice*,

The servants – from chambermaid to under-keeper – know what's going on. They recognise the signs, and act . . . accordingly. There is, therefore, the sense that the servants who silently watch and know, represent the 'real life' that infringes on the fantasy *mise-en-scène* of the woman's picture.[26]

This contrast is made explicit in *Far from Heaven* in the scene in which Sybil is revealed to have a social life away from the Whitakers. In an echo of a sequence from Sirk's *Imitation of Life*, Cathy – spurred to action by her relationship with Raymond – asks Sybil about the church group of which she is a member. Sybil mentions several organisations, surprising Cathy. ('I think that's marvellous, Sybil, that you even find the time.') Cathy offers a donation: 'We just have so much up in the attic I've been meaning to go through.' Opening the door to leave, she is door-stepped by a young black couple from the NAACP. Cathy politely brushes them off as she is 'terribly late' for her daughter's ballet recital, leaving Sybil to sign a roster. Cathy's patronising token gesture of political and moral support – recycled goods from her loft, a sanctioned system of hand-me-downs for the needy – is clearly differentiated from actual political engagement. (To be fair, Cathy does later phone the NAACP to offer her services as a volunteer – though the call is interrupted by Frank returning home to announce he has fallen for another man.)

It is never made clear whether Sybil has children or a family. This omission means, in White's words, that she represents 'a deviation from heterosexualised femininity'. Further, her relationship with Cathy crosses a racial boundary, which inflects the sexual and power dynamic between them. As White writes,

The complexity, code crossing, and incoherence of racialized sexual and gender ideology is performed by the on-screen conjunction of, and contrast between, black and white women. The mammy stereotype, often denounced as 'asexual', may be inflected as 'lesbian' in its close articulation with the presentation of the white heroine's desire [. . .] A process of erotic doubling between a woman of colour and the white star may also serve to figure lesbianism . . . Or the racist projection of sexuality onto the 'other woman' may indicate erotic tension between the stereotyped woman of colour and the 'repressed' and only presumptively heterosexual white heroine.[27]

Sybil is not a 'mammy' figure – Viola Davis is the wrong shape for such a type, and plays the role as quiet and deferential rather than blowsy. And the interactions between Cathy and Sybil are far from fractious, confrontational or even sparky; the queer boss/housekeeper dynamics of *The Servant* (Losey, 1963) or *Sister My Sister* (Meckler, 1994) are not in evidence. Lynne Joyrich does suggest that Sybil and Cathy can be seen as the 'primary couple' in *Far from Heaven*, but concludes that 'this relationship [is] one that can only be approached by allusion,' and that the film is ultimately 'unable to narrate this possibility'.[28] However, Sybil's power, afforded to her by the knowledge she accrues through quietly watching, taken in tandem with her racial difference from Cathy, position the character queerly, imbued with a potential that – if she had Mona's scruples and penchant for wanton behaviour – could easily be unleashed.

Queer Theory: Retrospective Readings

A third argument regarding *Far from Heaven*'s queerness relates to the film's impact on audience understandings of classical melodrama. As has been noted in previous chapters, Todd Haynes's film is not simply a direct simulation of Sirk's style and form, as he has injected particular elements – overt homosexuality, most notably – that almost never appeared in the 1950s movies. This inclusion has an effect on how audiences subsequently re-view classical melodramas. In keeping with arguments put forward by specific queer theorists regarding the practices of queer reading, *Far from Heaven* revisits extant work and guides viewers to do the same. That is, Haynes's film invites audiences to rewatch classical melodramas and to perceive absences, elisions and codes previously overlooked, as well as to explore their individual emotional and psychological relationships with specific films.

As outlined in the first section of this chapter, queer reading practices have provided a consistent topic of exploration in queer film theory. A foundational approach is posited in Alexander Doty's *Making Things Perfectly Queer*, in which he explores the queerness of a range of historically situated popular culture texts, including *Laverne and Shirley* and *The Jack Benny Program*. Crucially, he insists that such a reading practice is not a perversion of any true and intended meaning, but rather the bringing to light of codes and content always already present. As he writes,

Queer readings aren't 'alternative' readings, wishful or wilful misreadings, or 'reading too much into things' readings. They result from the recognition and articulation of the complex range of queerness that has been in popular culture texts and their audiences all along.[29]

This perspective has subsequently informed a significant number of queer theoretical writings on individual films and television programmes.

Many of the essays on specific films in Ellis Hanson's edited volume *Out Takes*, for example, describe and explore identifiably queer content and contexts previously ignored or marginalised.[30]

A more complex model of queer reading of historical film texts has been outlined in Patricia White's book *Uninvited*. White puts forward the concept of 'retrospectatorship', in an attempt to account for the ways in which contemporary viewers engage with classical Hollywood movies – in particular, the ability of spectators to look back at those films and examine the ways in which their meanings and significance have become constituted over time and in retrospect. As she notes, the fact that 'classical Hollywood cinema belongs to the past but is experienced in a present that affords us new ways of seeing' enables film spectators to consider the impact of that historical lag or gap.[31] For White, any consideration of this relationship – between the spectator in the present and the film made in a different historical period – must of necessity confront the workings of memory and fantasy, and the ways in which audiences psychologically relate to film history. As she writes, 'all spectatorship, insofar as it engages subjective fantasy, revises memory traces and experiences, some of which are memories and experiences of other movies.'[32]

One of the main effects achieved by *Far from Heaven* is that, in referencing key melodramatic films so directly and explicitly – an extensive list of movies quoted from or alluded to was outlined in Chapter 2 – audiences are asked to reconsider those films, and in particular their lack of gay characters and plots. Was the expulsion of queerness from those films, or its banishing to the margins, entirely successful? Or can we now revisit those movies and read their absences and omissions in new ways? Laura Mulvey, in her review of *Far from Heaven*, concludes that this is one of the major achievements of Haynes's film. Comparing its plot and content with *The Reckless Moment*, she observes that:

The two stories come together at the end. Cathy lies on her bed, crying for her lost love, and at the cruelty of their world, just as Lucia Harper in the same *mise en scène* weeps for the petty criminal who had fallen in love with her. In both movies the telephone rings and Sybil calls out 'Mr Harper/Mr Whitaker on the telephone, Mrs Harper/Mrs Whitaker!' Here the films diverge. In *Far from Heaven*, a cutaway shot shows Frank talking on the telephone in his hotel room, with his lover in the background. Of course, there's no such cutaway in *The Reckless Moment*. But the fan of the Hollywood melodrama cannot but pick up the implications behind Haynes' suggestion. Tom Harper's absence from the family might well be due to other reasons apart from engineering work in Berlin. While *Far from Heaven* can be appreciated on any level, these cross-narrative implications, poignant and witty, suggest that now that cinema is history, the film-maker can also be the film historian.[33]

In other words, *Far from Heaven* provokes its viewers to return to the films it quotes and pick apart their content. Of course, the McGehee/Siegel remake of *The Reckless Moment, The Deep End* (2001), has a similar sort of effect: in reconfiguring the son as gay, the new version implies queerness was excised from the original. However, *The Reckless Moment* is just one of the many films alluded to by *Far from Heaven*. In addition, Haynes's sustained adoption of an outmoded style (a tactic avoided by the makers of *The Deep End*) also opens up questions about spectatorial relationships, psychic and emotional, with particular filmic aesthetics from the past.

Following Mulvey's argument, *Far from Heaven*'s content also has an impact on the re-viewing of other movies to which it alludes. Jonathan Rosenbaum has suggested that Frank Whitaker's fury at his inability to summon an erection recalls similar raging by Kyle Hadley (Robert Stack) in *Written on the Wind*.[34] This provokes viewers to rewatch Sirk's film and query the sexual orientation of Stack's character. What lies behind his neurosis – and his claustrophobically close friendship with Mitch Wayne (Rock Hudson)? Why does his marriage not function and what hidden emotions are working themselves out in his violence? Similarly, the allusions to Ophüls's *Letter from an Unknown Woman* – evident in *Far from Heaven*'s farewell at the train station and the circular form of its narrative, Dana Luciano argues[35] – provoke retrospective analysis of the earlier film. Other than the intervening gaps of years, why is the pianist Stefan (Louis Jourdan) unable to remember Lisa (Joan Fontaine) each time he meets her? Although Lisa has a child by Stefan, the result of one of their few brief times together, the snarls and tangles of the plot that prevent the two from coming together as a couple, and the span of decades the narrative covers, produce significant lacunae and gaps in their tale. This is not to suggest that Stefan's character is a homosexual (though his over-investment in his collection of musical instruments could be read in such a way); rather, it is to suggest that there is something queer in the cat-and-mouse dynamic of their relationship and in their failure to attain a blissful, normative heterosexual union. As a third and final example, Dan Sallitt has suggested a connection between Haynes's film and Preminger's *Bunny Lake is Missing*.[36] This is

most apparent, arguably, in the multiple conservative forces that conspire to cause grief for a central couple, as well as in the film's perverse
supporting characters. (Noel Coward's landlord in Preminger's film,
tiny dog in hand, is even fruitier than Mona's gay uncle.) As in *Far from
Heaven*, the 'couple' in *Bunny Lake* – Ann Lake (Carol Lynley) and her
brother Stephen (Keir Dullea) – also crack under the strain; like Frank,
Stephen has a hidden identity that is eventually exposed. He is actually a
kidnapper, responsible for the disappearance of his niece, but an oblique
approach to the film easily configures him as queer; Stephen is a pretty
young man, with an inappropriate emotional fixation on a bad object
(his sister). Does the revelation of his criminality, the peeling back of his
respectable surface, actually cover over another facet of his identity?

When Cathy and Raymond have their 'break-up' conversation
outside of the cinema, she asks him 'Do you think we ever really do
see beyond . . . the surface of things?' *Far from Heaven* explores the ten-
sions and discrepancies between pristine public surface and that which
lies beneath: hidden emotions and passions, closeted identities and the
truthful nature of relationships. In addition, it critiques the morality
of judgements and opinions made on the scant evidence of appearance: hastily jumped-to conclusions which spread as wildfire rumour;
small-town racism grounded in ignorance and an antipathy towards
non-white skin colours. And yet at an additional remove, Cathy's question is posed to the spectator of melodramas. Looking back at examples
of classical Hollywood cinema, are viewers dazzled by the surface –
production design, beautiful stars, sumptuous score – and thus blinded
to undercurrents, elisions and the marginal or hidden? *Far from Heaven*
works not only as a work of retrospectatorship, or queer reading, on the
films it directly quotes. It also coaxes viewers to look similarly askance
at other melodramatic films from the same era, and asks: what queer
content or register have you been ignoring? And how might that have
affected your emotional and psychological relationship with those films
as you have rewatched them during your life?

Far from Heaven as an AIDS Movie

The fourth argument to be made regarding the queerness of *Far from
Heaven* relates to the film's status as an HIV/AIDS movie. A significant
percentage of writings by gay, lesbian and queer cinema theorists have
explored films that directly or indirectly tackle HIV/AIDS. As was

identified in Chapter 2, this is one element that binds together many of the films of Todd Haynes – especially *Superstar*, *Poison* and *Safe*, with their sick and wasting characters. At first appraisal, *Far from Heaven* might seem difficult to categorise as an AIDS film; the 1950s setting prefigures the identification and spread of HIV. However, looked at more obliquely – that is to say, queerly – there are a number of ways in which the film can be read as handling this topic.

The only 'sick' character in *Far from Heaven*, at least according to prominent medical and cultural discourses of the era, is Frank. As he says, when visiting the doctor, 'I can't let this thing destroy my life – my family's life! I *know* it's a sickness because it makes me feel despicable, dirty.' However, Frank's homosexuality is not a simple allegory for HIV/AIDS. He experiences psychological difficulties in reconciling himself to his orientation but is not physically ill; he 'gets better', in that he comes to terms with his 'condition'. Indeed, we never see Frank return to the doctor, and he ends the movie separated from Cathy, with the promise of happiness with a male lover. This narrative arc is typical of the melodrama genre: a character becomes ill, goes through treatment, and either recovers or dies. In *Magnificent Obsession*, Helen Phillips (Jane Wyman) loses her sight but ultimately recovers it; in *Dark Victory* (Goulding, 1939), Judith Traherne (Bette Davis) is diagnosed with a brain tumour which eventually kills her.[37]

Many of the films that are centrally concerned with HIV/AIDS, whether mainstream, independent or European art-house, adopt a melodramatic form. This can be observed in, for instance, *Buddies* (Bressan, Jr, 1985), *An Early Frost* (Erman, 1985), *Longtime Companion* (René, 1989), *Les Nuits fauves/Savage Nights* (Collard, 1992), *Philadelphia* (Jonathan Demme, 1993), *The Last Supper* (Roberts, 1994) and *It's My Party* (Kleiser, 1996). It also applies to a number of films in which HIV/AIDS appears as a plot facet, if not a central one, including *Peter's Friends* (Branagh, 1992), *Love! Valour! Compassion!* (Mantello, 1997), *All About My Mother* and *The Hours* (Daldry, 2002). *Far from Heaven* shares elements with many of these films, especially the bringing together of homosexuality, a mysterious and poorly comprehended 'sickness', a search for a cure, and cold or unsympathetic doctors. But there are other narrative components that connect Haynes's film to those more overtly about HIV/AIDS: sexual interactions that have to be broken off or interrupted, causing emotional distress; a party which attempts to cover over manifold miseries; a recognition that conventional social structures, including the family, will struggle to understand and accommodate 'abnormality'.

In a number of scenes throughout *Far from Heaven*, various ways of describing, categorising and comprehending homosexuality are presented. In the film's opening minutes, Frank is branded a 'loiterer' by the police, after being arrested for cruising. Eleanor's conversation with Cathy about Mona's uncle makes use of euphemisms and the correct descriptor; later, she implies that Frank's homosexuality might be infectious, or at least a negative influence to be kept away from children. When Frank visits Dr Bowman to discuss a cure, he is informed that, for 'this sort of behaviour', there 'remains only a scant, 5 to 30 percent rate of success, for complete heterosexual conversion'. Bowman identifies Frank's condition as not 'normal', but implies that it is innate, essential and very difficult to alter, except 'when it's what the patient himself desires more than anything else in the world'. As was noted in Chapter 2, this interest in the cultural and institutional discourses that attempt to explain the abnormal connects *Far from Heaven* to some of Haynes's earlier films, especially *Superstar*, *Poison* and *Safe*.

Those social, cultural and sanctioned discourses also impact on Cathy, of course, and prevent her from forging a relationship with Raymond. Cathy is almost always under surveillance, and struggles to find anywhere to be alone with her gardener. At her home, they are observed by Sybil; at Ernie's, they are spotted by Mona, and Raymond is confronted by a patron; they are coerced out of a diner by the waiter; when Cathy places her hand on Raymond's arm outside the cinema, he is shouted at by a passer-by ('You! Boy! Hands off!'); at Raymond's house, they have to meet at a side door. Only at the pond in the woods do they spend time alone, away from the eyes of others. In comparison, Frank's meetings with other men – in his office late at night, cruising at a cinema, in a gay bar, in his hotel room while on holiday – are relatively easy and discrete, and mostly conducted in private and secluded spaces. The characters in *Far from Heaven* even struggle to describe exactly what is going on between Cathy and Raymond, as though articulating an inter-racial romance is almost impossible. The content of Mona's gossip is never presented directly, but Eleanor tells Cathy that Mona claims 'she saw *you* and a *coloured* man, somewhere out on Franklin, coming out of a truck or some such thing,' those last nebulous words hinting at something more intimate than mere socialising. Later, when Cathy tells Eleanor about her friendship with Raymond, she says 'We would

just talk. But somehow it made me feel – oh, I don't know. Alive somewhere.' Although Cathy often struggles with words in *Far from Heaven*,
the tone of her voice, the glow in her face, her position looking up and
out of the window, and the vague phrases, 'I don't know', 'somewhere',
make clear the depth of her feeling without articulating specifics.

For Amy Taubin, it is the cultural and institutional forces that exert
pressure on Frank, Cathy and Raymond that enable an understanding
of *Far from Heaven* as an AIDS film. Indeed, she interprets the movie as
a critical commentary on the continued power of conservative forces in
the United States:

Just as *Safe* was a response to the AIDS crisis in which the term AIDS went
unmentioned, *Far from Heaven* is a furious denunciation of the return to rampant
power of the military-industrial complex and its fat-cat frontmen, hawking their
medicine show elixir of patriotism, religion, and family values, the side effects of
which are anxiety, suspicion and full-blown paranoia.[38]

If the actions and protests of ACT-UP, Gran Fury and other queer activist groups in the late 1980s and early 1990s directly targeted big business,
politicians, the medical and legal systems, and so on, then the content of
Far from Heaven can be read as a subtle echo of those activities. Haynes's
film clearly identifies the misery caused to the three lead characters by
the forces of conservative thought and action – Cathy, in particular,
is left ruined and alone. However, as Fassbinder wrote, 'Never mind
if a film ends pessimistically; if it explores certain mechanisms clearly
enough to show people exactly how they work, then the ultimate effect is
not pessimistic.'[39] Audiences may leave the film and its downbeat ending
consoling themselves that social and cultural conditions improved in the
decades following the 1950s; however, Haynes is actually asking whether
things really have significantly progressed in the intervening years.

Far from Heaven's pessimistic conclusion, which leaves Cathy separated
from Frank and waving goodbye to any chance of a relationship with
Raymond, may leave audiences in tears. As was explored in Chapter 3,
the affective impact of *Far from Heaven* is complex to unpack. The tears
that it provokes from some viewers may be due to the standard narrative
dynamics of melodrama: the relationship between audience knowledge
and that of the characters, the timing of particular plot events and revelations. In addition, they may be caused by nostalgia, both for an earlier
period in history, and for films like those made by Sirk. As Richard Dyer
has noted,

What happens in the film is sad but we may also be sad for there not being films that do sadness like this anymore [. . .] There is something about the difficulty of emotion in 1950s melodrama, not least in its interface with social expectation, that gives it a special intensity, and it seems a cultural loss no longer to have this at one's disposal.[40]

An additional way to understand this sense of sadness is to frame it in relation to mourning. Dyer's description suggests that contemporary viewers of *Far from Heaven* may mourn the loss of a particular mode of film practice, and in particular the 'unaffected, unalloyed, unironic emotional intensity in the depiction of interpersonal relationships'[41] found in movies by Sirk and others.

Of course, mourning is not an emotional experience particular to gay men or queers. However, in relation to HIV/AIDS, mourning took on a particular political valence for those affected by the disease. Critics including Douglas Crimp have identified the ways in which the public expression of grief by people affected by HIV/AIDS, particularly in the face of ignorance or condemnation by powerful and conservative bodies (the medical profession, various religious groups, and so on), was a critically important practice.[42] Mourning the dead and lost in conspicuous ways, through strategies such as the Names Project Memorial Quilt, became fundamentally important in raising the visibility of an illness that many wanted to shun or disregard. As Jeff Nunokawa wrote in 1991,

Homophobia has seldom been more obtrusive than in its current disinclination to allow the gay community to grieve its own publicly; seldom more annoying than in its refusal to honour an exigency of expression as compelling as hunger, anger, or fear; seldom plainer than in the harassment and repression, variously violent and squeamish, institutional and intimate, by which it has worked to make the casualties of the present crisis disappear. The understated, understood, remedial urgency of efforts of remembrance such as the Names Project, efforts of remembrance that emerge from the gay community itself, describes a pressure that persistently attends the work of remembering such casualties, a pressure to mark deaths that the majority culture is simply not disposed to notice.[43]

Far from Heaven is a movie made by a gay man and former AIDS activist in the wake of HIV/AIDS; its narrative takes place in a decade before the disease. Many films that directly deal with HIV/AIDS overtly mourn for the time before the disease. *Longtime Companion* ends with a fantasy reunion sequence set on a beach, those friends and lovers lost to AIDS suddenly returned and healthy; *Philadelphia* concludes with the family of Andy (Tom Hanks) watching home videos of him when he was a healthy child. Any contemporary film about homosexuality set in a time prior to the 1980s is, by default, an AIDS film in that it depicts a period before the illness first manifested.

Of course, Frank's narrative may be difficult to endure for queer viewers, depicting as it does subterranean bars, clandestine meetings, and feelings of shame and guilt – what Dolly Parton might have called 'the good old days, when times were bad'. And yet a number of queer theorists have critically explored contemporary yearnings – nostalgic, mournful – for that lost time, and the associated emotional turmoil (or otherwise) experienced then by queer people.[44] Others have interrogated the significance of queer shame, including its political ramifications, and the importance of experiencing the emotion.[45] Despite some trauma, Frank's story ends relatively positively, and he is the only character in *Far from Heaven* who has sex (though all that is shown is foreplay in his office and seduction in the hotel room). Haynes invites his queer viewers to mourn the passing of the 1950s, positioning Frank's experience of his sexual orientation as typical, even emblematic of the period. And yet, as with its depiction of crushing conservative forces, *Far from Heaven* also invites spectators to reflect on how much has changed: are Frank's experiences of shame so different to those of many contemporary queers struggling to come to terms with their feelings?

Conclusion

This chapter has presented a range of different ways to think about *Far from Heaven* as a queer film. Despite the fairly strict adherence of the movie to generic conventions established in the 1950s – with some minor variations in terms of style and content – the film also has the potential to be seen as politically significant, nowhere more so than in its handling of queer themes, subjects and approaches. Four particular topics have been explored by this chapter: how *Far from Heaven* employs and references elements adopted from queer 'underground', 'independent' and 'art-house' revisions to the melodrama, thus perverting the mainstream; supporting characters, and the queer register that they can bring to a film's narrative; the retrospective subversive readings of classical melodrama that *Far from Heaven* invites audiences to undertake subsequently; and the ways in which Haynes's film can be understood as concerned with, or related to, HIV/AIDS. Although other approaches could have been explored – unpacking the film's uses of colour, for example – the subjects explored here offer models for how queer theory can open up *Far from Heaven* in ways that reveal its complexity, subtlety and significance.

Coda

Todd Haynes's next feature film after *Far from Heaven* was *I'm Not There* (2007), in which six different actors play facets of Bob Dylan's character and history. Haynes had previously had trouble obtaining music rights for his films *Superstar: The Karen Carpenter Story* and *Velvet Goldmine*; the distribution of the former was blocked by the Carpenter estate for unapproved use of a number of songs, and David Bowie refused to let the director use his music in the latter. Dylan, however, approved the use of his songs in *I'm Not There*. Made for around $20 million, Haynes's largest budget to date, the finances were assembled through a number of different sources, including Endgame Entertainment, Rising Star and John Wells Productions. Filming began in July 2006, with the completed cut premiering at the Telluride Film Festival in August 2007. The film returned Haynes to the multi-strand narrative format of *Poison*, and to the music biopic genre first experimented with in *Superstar*; it arguably served as his most sustained engagement to date with the notion of identity as a performance, a cultural construction that can be shaped and altered. As he has said,

The minute you try to grab hold of Dylan, he's no longer where he was. He's like a flame: if you try to hold him in your hand you'll surely get burned. Dylan's life of change and constant disappearances and constant transformations makes you yearn to hold him, and to nail him down. And that's why his fan base is so obsessive, so desirous of finding the truth and the absolutes and the answers to him – things that Dylan will never provide and will only frustrate . . . Dylan is difficult and mysterious and evasive and frustrating, and it only makes you identify with him all the more as he skirts identity.[1]

Despite some positive reviews, *I'm Not There* performed rather poorly at the box office, taking just $4 million in the United States and around $7.5 million overseas. Distributed by the Weinstein Company, presumably following some patching-up of differences between Haynes and Harvey Weinstein, the film's widest release in US cinemas had it on 149 screens (half that of *Far from Heaven*). A number of critics, including Todd McCarthy in *Variety*, noted that *I'm Not There* is predominantly for specialists – that is, fans of Dylan.[2] Certainly, other than the strand of the film in which Cate Blanchett plays Dylan, queer fans of Haynes might have been searching for the director's usual politics – for something more 'flaming' than 'flame'.

Haynes's career, as identified in Chapter 1 of this book, has oscillated between melodramas focused on female protagonists (*Superstar*, *Safe*, *Far from Heaven*) and those centred on men (*Poison*, *Velvet Goldmine*, *I'm Not There*). Continuing this trend in a neat pattern, Haynes completed shooting a five-hour adaptation of *Mildred Pierce* for the US TV channel HBO in August 2010. Although I briefly suggested that *Far from Heaven* could be conceptualised as a work of adaptation in Chapter 2 of this book, *Mildred Pierce* is Haynes's first adaptation from a source novel. Returning to the original James M. Cain book from 1941, the script was co-written by Jonathan Raymond and Haynes. Raymond was one of the two authors of the screenplay for *Old Joy* (Reichardt, 2007), a film which Haynes executive produced. Haynes's adaptation features Kate Winslet as Mildred, Evan Rachel Wood as her daughter Veda, and Guy Pearce as love interest Monty. Several of the personnel that Haynes worked with on *Far from Heaven* were also involved in making *Mildred Pierce*, including producers Christine Vachon and John Wells, cinematographer Edward Lachman and production designer Mark Friedberg. Ilene Landress, producer of *The Sopranos*, and Killer Films' Pamela Koffler also acted as producers for the adaptation.

Mildred Pierce was previously adapted for the screen in 1945, directed by Michael Curtiz and starring Joan Crawford as the titular protagonist; it was the only film for which Crawford won the Academy Award for Best Actress. The Curtiz version differed from the Cain book on account of restrictions imposed by the Hays Code; the semi-incestuous romance between Monty and his step-daughter Veda, for instance, was toned down, whereas the amount of violence was increased. *Mildred Pierce* skilfully combined the genres of noir and melodrama, the tribulations of a single mother with two children giving way to a murder plot. Without the restrictions of the Production Code to contend with, Haynes's version has the potential to be more faithful to its rather perverse source, and to place more emphasis on the melodrama than the noir.

That *Mildred Pierce* was made for television, rather than cinema, is not surprising. As noted in Chapter 3, it has often been argued that the genre of the melodrama migrated from cinemas to television from the 1960s onwards, with the soap opera adopting or adapting many of the constituent components of the classical family melodrama for domestic viewing. Certainly, despite the best efforts of the gay/queer directors who sent a flurry of melodramas into cinemas in the first years of the twenty-first century, attempting to revive the genre, it remains mostly elusive on the big screen. Aside from the occasional title – *Dear John*, perhaps the adaptation of Jodi Picoult's novel *My Sister's Keeper* (Nick Cassavetes, 2009) – melodrama of the classical 'tearjerker' form is now largely a historical genre, a way that audiences used to watch.

In relation to that flurry, Haynes's film now seems especially like one of a kind, its wholesale simulation of Sirkian style largely faithful to genre trappings, and offering a heartfelt alternative to the campy pastiche of *Moulin Rouge!* and *8 Women*, or the complex multi-strand narrative of *The Hours*. As this book has demonstrated, beneath its seemingly simple, seamless recreation of an earlier form of filmmaking, Haynes's film tackles seriously a large number of substantial questions – about authorship, about the persistence or loss of melodrama as a genre, about the queerness of particular narrative devices, and so on. Other gay and queer directors have subsequently made period dramas with queer content, including *Savage Grace* (Kalin, 2007) and *A Single Man* (Ford, 2009), but none of these operates strictly within the restraints of the classical melodrama. Looked at historically, *Far from Heaven* is genuinely unique and idiosyncratic. And in the final analysis, it is perhaps this uniqueness that most clearly marks *Far from Heaven* as a truly independent film.

Notes

Introduction

1. Gleiberman, 2002, internet; Sterritt, 2002, internet.
2. Falcon, 2003, p. 12.
3. For further discussion of *Poison*'s reception, see Wyatt, 1998a, pp. 35–48. Lisa Duggan and Nan D. Hunter's *Sex Wars* (1995) outlines crucial political and cultural contexts in operation in the United States at the time of *Poison*'s making and release.
4. Rich, 1992, pp. 32–5.
5. Vachon, 2006, p. 152. For further detail of *Velvet Goldmine*'s production, see Vachon, 1998.
6. Taylor, 2002, internet.
7. Sullivan, 2007, internet.
8. Haynes quoted in Taylor, 2002, internet.
9. Vachon, 2006, p. 153.
10. Vachon, 2006, pp. 153–4.
11. Haynes, director's commentary, *Far from Heaven* DVD.
12. Haynes, 2003a, pp. 99–100.

Chapter 1

1. Kleinhans, 1998, p. 311.
2. For a comprehensive history of independent film production in the United States, see Tzioumakis, 2006.
3. Kleinhans, 1998, p. 308.
4. King, 2005, p. 2.
5. Ibid., p. 19.
6. For a full list of these companies, see Tzioumakis, 2006, p. 258.
7. King, 2005, p. 22.

8. Rosen, 1990, p. 264.
9. Wyatt, 1998b, p. 74.
10. Pierson, 1997, pp. 126–32.
11. Wyatt, 1998b, p. 80.
12. Ibid., p. 81.
13. Tzioumakis, 2006, pp. 261–2.
14. King, 2009, p. 240. For a more detailed history of the development of Focus Features, see Needham, 2010, pp. 12–19.
15. King, 2009, p. 240.
16. Needham, 2010, p. 17.
17. Ibid.
18. Tzioumakis, 2006, pp. 247–8.
19. Holmlund, 2005, p. 1.
20. Ibid., p. 9.
21. *Obselidia* screened at the Edinburgh International Film Festival in 2010; the information in this paragraph is taken from a Q&A session with Diane Bell that accompanied the screening.
22. Tzioumakis, 2006, p. 6.
23. All figures are taken from www.boxofficemojo.com.
24. Kleinhans, 1998, p. 317.
25. Tzioumakis, 2006, pp. 275–7; Dobuzinskis, 2008, internet.
26. Hoberman and Rosenbaum, 1983, pp. 214–51.
27. Rich, 2005, pp. 32–5.
28. Vachon, 2006, p. 159.
29. Ibid.
30. Ibid., p. 161.
31. Needham, 2010, p. 13.
32. Vachon, 2006, p. 160.
33. James, 2003, p. 15.
34. Vachon, 2006, p. 159.
35. Haynes, director's commentary on *Far from Heaven* DVD.
36. Vachon, 2006, p. 178.
37. Ibid., p. 180.
38. Ibid., pp. 39–40.
39. Hebron, 2003, internet.
40. Negra, 2005, p. 82.
41. Vachon, 2006, p. 172.
42. Ibid., p. 156.
43. Ibid., p. 162.

44. Ibid., p. 156.
45. Ibid., p. 164.
46. Ibid., p. 164.
47. King, 2009, p. 7.
48. Higson, 1991, p. 161, p. 162.
49. Waters, 1991, p. 180.
50. King, 2005, p. 111.
51. Ibid., p. 110.
52. James, 2003, p. 14.
53. Haynes in 'Anatomy of a Scene', *Far from Heaven* DVD extra.
54. Haynes in 'The Making of *Far from Heaven*', *Far from Heaven* DVD extra.
55. Julianne Moore in 'Anatomy of a Scene', *Far from Heaven* DVD extra.
56. Dargis, 2002.
57. O'Brien, 2002, p. 202.
58. Tzioumakis, 2006, p. 6.
59. Haynes, quoted in O'Brien, 2002, p. 156.
60. Ibid.
61. Higgins, 2007, p. 102.
62. Ibid.
63. Ibid.
64. Haynes, director's commentary on *Far from Heaven* DVD.
65. Haynes, 'Anatomy of a Scene', *Far from Heaven* DVD extra.
66. Mark Friedberg, 'Anatomy of a Scene', *Far from Heaven* DVD extra.
67. Haynes quoted in O'Brien, 2002, p. 155.
68. Lyons, 1994; Levy, 1999.
69. King, 2005, p. 199.
70. Willis, 2003, p. 135.
71. Klinger, 1994, pp. 149–51.
72. Mulvey, 2003, p. 40.

Chapter 2

1. Andrew, 1998, p. 3.
2. Cameron, 1981 [1962], p. 52.
3. Moverman, 1996, p. 231.
4. Morrison, 2007a, p. 133.
5. Haynes, 2003b, pp. viii–ix.
6. Uhlich, 2002, internet.
7. Doane, 2004, p. 17.

8. Eco, 1989 [1962]; Barthes, 1981 [1968]. See also Derrida 2001 [1967].
9. Deleuze and Guattari, 2004a [1972]; Foucault 1991 [1975], 1998 [1976]. See also Deleuze and Guattari, 2004b [1980].
10. Arroyo, 1993, pp. 72–98.
11. Taubin, 1996, p. 32.
12. Morrison, 2007b, p. 1.
13. Hunter, 2002, internet.
14. Morrison, 2007a, p. 138.
15. Baudrillard, 1994 [1981], pp. 45–6.
16. Jameson, 1991, pp. 16–17.
17. Morrison, 2007a, pp. 138–9.
18. Horsley, 2008, internet.
19. Dyer, 1991, p. 196.
20. Barthes, 1981 [1968]; Foucault, 1977.
21. Dyer, 1991, p. 186.
22. Ibid., pp. 187–8.
23. Staiger, 2004, pp. 1–22.
24. Rosenbaum, 1998, internet.
25. See, for instance, Doty, 1993, pp. 17–38.
26. Halliday, 1997, p. 140.
27. Rosenbaum, 2002, internet; Sallitt, n.d., internet.
28. Haynes, 'Introduction', DVD extra on *The Reckless Moment*.
29. This point is also made by Laura Mulvey in her review of *Far from Heaven* for *Sight and Sound* (2003, pp. 40–1).
30. Haynes, director's commentary on *Far from Heaven* DVD.
31. Luciano, 2007, p. 265.
32. Haynes, director's commentary, *Far from Heaven* DVD.
33. Sallitt, n.d., internet.
34. This connection is also highlighted by Richard Dyer (2007, p. 175).
35. Joyrich, 2004, p. 192.
36. O'Brien, 2002, p. 154.
37. Hoberman, 2002, internet.
38. Hayward, 2006, p. 265.
39. Rhodes, 2007, p. 70.
40. Jameson, 1991, p. 32 and p. 17.
41. Hutcheon, 1989, p. 94.
42. Dyer, 2007, pp. 179–80.
43. Ibid., p. 180.

Chapter 3

1. Davis, 2008, pp. 43–61.
2. Elsaesser, 1987, p. 44, p. 45.
3. Gledhill, 1987, p. 17.
4. Singer, 1990, p. 95.
5. Neale, 1993.
6. Elsaesser, 1987, p. 62.
7. Mercer and Shingler, 2004, pp. 12–13.
8. Haynes, 2003b, p. xi.
9. Elsaesser, 1987, p. 55.
10. Haynes, director's commentary on *Far from Heaven* DVD. The voice-over dialogue can be found in the *Far from Heaven* published screenplay: Haynes, 2003a, pp. 99–100.
11. Elsaesser, 1987, p. 50.
12. 'Anatomy of a Scene', *Far from Heaven* DVD extra.
13. James, 2003, p. 15.
14. Nowell-Smith, 1987, p. 73.
15. Klinger, 1994, pp. 148–9.
16. Haynes, 2003a, p. 30, p. 74.
17. Gledhill, 1987, p. 34.
18. For further exploration of these complexities, see Hallam and Marshment, 2000.
19. Elsaesser, 1987, p. 64.
20. Taylor, 2002, internet.
21. See, for instance: Hilderbrand, 2002, internet; Falcon, 2003; Taylor, 2002, internet.
22. Dyer, 2007, p. 175.
23. Dargis, 2002.
24. Mendelsohn, 2003, internet.
25. Gledhill, 1987, p. 5.
26. Mulvey, 1987.
27. Halliday, 1997, is an expanded edition of the original 1971 publication.
28. Camper, 1971; Halliday 1971; Willemen, 1971.
29. Halliday and Mulvey (eds), 1972.
30. Reprinted as Elsaesser 1987.
31. Klinger, 1994, p. 18.
32. See, for instance, Nowell-Smith, 1977, reprinted as Nowell-Smith 1987.

33. Haynes, 2003c, p. xiv.
34. Vachon, 2006, p. 170.
35. Halliday, 1997, pp. 106–7.
36. Haynes, quoted in Taylor, 2002, internet.
37. Haynes, quoted in Kaufman, 2002, internet.
38. O'Hehir, 2002, internet.
39. Dyer, 2007, p. 174.
40. Neale, 1986, p. 7.
41. Moretti, quoted in Neale, 1986, p. 8.
42. Neale, 1986, p. 11, p. 12.
43. Frith, 1984, p. 83.
44. See, for instance, Jeff Smith, 1999.
45. Plantinga, 1999, p. 245.
46. Doane, 2004, p. 10.
47. Ibid., p. 5.
48. Ibid., p. 13.
49. Neale, 1986, p. 22.
50. Oliver, 1993.
51. Warhol, 2003, p. 31.
52. Moore, quoted in Tobias, 2008, internet. A Youtube video entitled 'Julianne Moore Loves to Cry' compiles moments of the actress weeping in her films. Online: http://www.youtube.com/watch?v=d4uv0eD5Ufg (accessed 23 December 2010).
53. Dyer, 2002a.
54. Cottingham, 2005, p. 26.
55. Rosenbaum, 2004, p. 334.
56. Halliday, 1997, p. 107.
57. Johnson, 2005.
58. In this regard, it is worth noting the recent announcement that *Far from Heaven* is to be made into a stage musical by Playwrights Horizons. See Healy, 2010, internet.
59. Finch and Kwietniowski, 1988, p. 73.
60. Mercer and Shingler, 2004, p. 106.
61. Dyer, 1986, p. 176.
62. Originally published in *Partisan Review* in 1964, 'Notes on "Camp"' was subsequently reprinted in Sontag, 1966.
63. Klinger, 1994, pp. 142–3.
64. Taylor, 2002, internet.
65. Shattuc, 1995, p. 101.

66. Farmer, 2000, p. 179.
67. Harris, 1999.
68. DeAngelis, 2001.

Chapter 4

1. This was not the first reclamation of the term 'queer', but it was certainly the most widespread; for earlier examples, see Chauncey, 1994.
2. Dyer, 2002b, pp. 6–7.
3. Sedgwick, 1993, p. 8.
4. Hall, 2003, p. 13.
5. These would include, as examples, a conference held in York, UK, in October 1992, which led to the publication *Activating Theory* (Bristow and Wilson, 1994), and the 1993 issue of *Signs: The Journal of Women in Culture and Society* devoted to 'Theorizing Lesbian Experience' (Volume 18, Number 4).
6. Spargo, 1999, p. 9.
7. Foucault, 1998 [1976]; Butler, 1990; Butler, 1993.
8. These writings would include: Dyer, 1977; Dyer, 1990; Russo, 1981; Tyler, 1972; Weiss, 1992; Wood, 1978.
9. Doty, 2000; Lang, 2002.
10. Terry, 1991.
11. La Bruce, 1995; DeAngelis, 2001; Whatling, 1997, pp. 134–59.
12. Mulvey, 1975.
13. Farmer, 2000, p. 25.
14. For example, see Stacey, 1992; Drukman, 1995.
15. Mayne, 1993, p. 97.
16. Farmer, 2000, pp. 38–9.
17. Smith, 1962–3.
18. Mercer and Shingler, 2004, pp. 110–11.
19. Ibid., p. 111.
20. See, for instance, Falcon, 2003; Willis, 2003.
21. Bronski, 1984, p. 102.
22. Roof, 2002, p. 3.
23. White, 1995, p. 93.
24. Ibid., 1995, p. 94.
25. Quoted in Simon, 2008, internet. Ellipsis in original.
26. Finch and Kwietniowski, 1988, p. 77.
27. White, 1995, p. 97.

28. Joyrich, 2004, p. 203.
29. Doty, 1993, p. 16.
30. Hanson (ed.), 1999.
31. White, 1999, p. 197.
32. Ibid., 1999, p. 197.
33. Mulvey, 2003, p. 41.
34. Rosenbaum, 2002, internet.
35. Luciano, 2007.
36. Sallitt, n.d., internet.
37. For a discussion of classical melodramas in which women are diagnosed as unwell and in need of treatment, see Doane, 1987, pp. 38–69.
38. Taubin, 2002, p. 26.
39. Fassbinder quoted in Haynes, 2003b, p. xii.
40. Dyer, 2007, p. 178.
41. Ibid.
42. Crimp, 2002.
43. Nunokawa, 1991, p. 319.
44. See, for instance, Love, 2009.
45. See, for example, Halperin and Traub (eds), 2010.

Coda

1. Haynes, quoted in Emerson, 2007, internet.
2. McCarthy, 2007, internet.

Bibliography

Andrew, Geoff (1998), *Stranger Than Paradise: Maverick Film-makers in Recent American Cinema*, London: Prion.

Arroyo, José (1993), 'Death, Desire and Identity: The Political Unconscious of "New Queer Cinema"' in Joseph Bristow and Angelia R. Wilson (eds), *Activating Theory: Lesbian, Gay, Bisexual Politics*, London: Lawrence & Wishart, pp. 72–98.

Barthes, Roland (1981 [1968]), 'The Death of the Author' in John Caughie (ed.), *Theories of Authorship*, London: Routledge & Kegan Paul, pp. 208–13.

Baudrillard, Jean (1994) [1981], *Simulacra and Simulations*, Ann Arbor: University of Michigan Press.

Bristow, Joseph and Angelia R. Wilson (eds) (1993), *Activating Theory: Lesbian, Gay, Bisexual Politics*, London: Lawrence & Wishart.

Bronski, Michael (1984), *Culture Clash: The Making of Gay Sensibility*, Boston: South End.

Butler, Judith (1990), *Gender Trouble*, London: Routledge.

Butler, Judith (1993), *Bodies that Matter: On the Discursive Limits of Sex*, London: Routledge.

Cameron, Ian (1981 [1962]), 'Films, Directors and Critics' in John Caughie (ed.), *Theories of Authorship*, London: Routledge & Kegan Paul, pp. 48–60.

Camper, Fred (1971), 'The Films of Douglas Sirk', *Screen*, Vol. 12, Issue 2 (Summer), pp. 44–62.

Chauncey, George (1994), *Gay New York: Gender, Urban Culture, and the Making of the Gay Male World, 1890–1940*, New York: HarperCollins.

Cottingham, Laura (2005), *Fear Eats the Soul*, London: BFI.

Crimp, Douglas (2002), *Melancholia and Moralism: Essays on AIDS and Queer Politics*, New York: MIT Press.

Dargis, Manohla (2002), review of *Far from Heaven*, *Los Angeles Times*, 8 November. Online: http://www.calendarlive.com/movies/reviews/cl-et-dargis8nov08,0,1566068.story (accessed 20 August 2010).

Davis, Glyn (2008), *Superstar: The Karen Carpenter Story*, New York: Wallflower.

DeAngelis, Michael (2001), *Gay Fandom and Crossover Stardom: James Dean, Mel Gibson and Keanu Reeves*, London: Duke University Press.

Deleuze, Gilles and Félix Guattari (2004a [1972]), *Anti-Oedipus*, New York: Continuum.

Deleuze, Gilles and Félix Guattari (2004b [1980]), *A Thousand Plateaus*, New York: Continuum.

Derrida, Jacques (2001 [1967]), 'Structure, Sign and Play in the Discourse of the Human Sciences' in Derrida, *Writing and Difference*, London: Routledge, pp. 351–70.

Doane, Mary Ann (1987), *The Desire to Desire: The Woman's Film of the 1940s*, Bloomington: Indiana University Press.

Doane, Mary Ann (2004), 'Pathos and Pathology: The Cinema of Todd Haynes', *Camera Obscura*, 57, Vol. 19, No. 3, pp. 1–21.

Dobuzinskis, Alex (2008), 'Just A Minute With: Kevin Smith on "Zack and Miri"'. Online: http://www.reuters.com/article/idUSTRE49T6SD20081030 (accessed 20 December 2010).

Doty, Alexander (1993), *Making Things Perfectly Queer: Interpreting Mass Culture*, Minneapolis: University of Minnesota Press.

Doty, Alexander (2000), *Flaming Classics: Queering the Film Canon*, London: Routledge.

Drukman, Steven (1995), 'The Gay Gaze, or Why I Want My MTV' in Paul Burston and Colin Richardson (eds), *A Queer Romance: Lesbians, Gay Men and Popular Culture*, London: Routledge, pp. 81–95.

Duggan, Lisa and Nan D. Hunter (eds) (1995), *Sex Wars: Sexual Dissent and Political Culture*, London: Routledge.

Dyer, Richard (ed.) (1977), *Gays and Film*, London: BFI.

Dyer, Richard (1986), *Heavenly Bodies: Film Stars and Society*, London: BFI.

Dyer, Richard (1990), *Now You See It: Studies on Lesbian and Gay Film*, London: Routledge.

Dyer, Richard (1991), 'Believing in Fairies: The Author and The Homosexual' in Diana Fuss (ed.), *Inside/Out: Lesbian Theories, Gay Theories*, London: Routledge, pp. 185–201.

Dyer, Richard (2002a), 'Seen to be Believed: Some Problems in the Representation of Gay People as Typical' in Dyer, *The Matter of Images: Essays on Representation*, London: Routledge, 2nd edn, pp. 19–49.

Dyer, Richard (2002b), 'Introduction' in Dyer, *The Culture of Queers*, London: Routledge, pp. 1–14.

Dyer, Richard (2007), *Pastiche*, London: Routledge.

Eco, Umberto (1989 [1962]), *The Open Work*, Cambridge, MA: Harvard University Press.

Elsaesser, Thomas (1987), 'Tales of Sound and Fury: Observations on the Family Melodrama' in Christine Gledhill (ed.), *Home is Where the Heart is: Studies in Melodrama and the Woman's Film*, London: BFI, pp. 43–69.

Emerson, Jim (2007), 'How Does it *Feel?* Footnote Fetishism and *I'm Not There*', *scanners::blog*, 9 October. Online: http://blogs.suntimes.com/scanners/2007/10/how_does_it_feel_footnote_feti.html (accessed 27 August 2010).

Falcon, Richard (2003), 'Magnificent Obsession', *Sight and Sound*, Vol. 13, No. 3 (March), pp. 12–15.

Farmer, Brett (2000), *Spectacular Passions: Cinema, Fantasy, Gay Male Spectatorships*, London: Duke University Press.

Finch, Mark and Richard Kwietniowski (1988), 'Melodrama and *Maurice*: Homo is Where the Het is', *Screen*, Vol. 29, Issue 3 (Summer), pp. 72–83.

Foucault, Michel (1977), 'What is an Author?' in Foucault, *Language, Counter-Memory, Practice: Selected Essays and Interviews*, Ithaca, NY: Cornell University Press, pp. 113–38.

Foucault, Michel (1991 [1975]), *Discipline and Punish: The Birth of the Prison*, London: Penguin.

Foucault, Michel (1998 [1976]), *The History of Sexuality, Volume 1: The Will to Knowledge*, London: Penguin.

Frith, Simon (1984), 'Mood Music: An Inquiry into Narrative Film Music', *Screen*, Vol. 25, Issue 3, pp. 78–88.

Gledhill, Christine (1987), 'The Melodramatic Field: An Investigation' in Gledhill (ed.), *Home is Where the Heart is: Studies in Melodrama and the Woman's Film*, London: BFI, pp. 5–39.

Gleiberman, Owen (2002), review of *Far from Heaven*, *Entertainment Weekly*, 30 October. Online: www.ew.com/ew/article/0,,385913~1~0~farfromheaven,00.html (accessed 26 August 2010).

Hall, Donald E. (2003), *Queer Theories*, Houndmills: Palgrave Macmillan.

Hallam, Julia and Margaret Marshment (2000), *Realism and Popular Cinema*, Manchester: Manchester University Press.

Halliday, Jon (1971), 'Notes on Sirk's German Films', *Screen*, Vol. 12, Issue 2 (Summer), pp. 8–14.

Halliday, Jon (1997), *Sirk on Sirk: Conversations with Jon Halliday*, London: Faber & Faber.

Halliday, Jon and Laura Mulvey (eds) (1972), *Douglas Sirk*, Edinburgh: Edinburgh Film Festival.

Halperin, David and Valerie Traub (eds) (2010), *Gay Shame*, Chicago: Chicago University Press.

Hanson, Ellis (ed.) (1999), *Out Takes: Essays on Queer Theory and Film*, London: Duke University Press.

Harris, Daniel (1999), *The Rise and Fall of Gay Culture*, New York: Ballantine.

Haynes, Todd (2003a), *Far from Heaven, Safe, Superstar: The Karen Carpenter Story: Three Screenplays*, New York: Grove.

Haynes, Todd (2003b), 'Three Screenplays: An Introduction' in Haynes, *Far from Heaven, Safe, Superstar: The Karen Carpenter Story: Three Screenplays*, New York: Grove, pp. vii–xii.

Haynes, Todd (2003c), 'Far from Heaven: Director's Statement' in Haynes, *Far from Heaven, Safe, Superstar: The Karen Carpenter Story: Three Screenplays*, New York: Grove, pp. xiii–xiv.

Hayward, Susan (2006), *Cinema Studies: The Key Concepts*, London: Routledge.

Healy, Patrick (2010), '"Grey Gardens" Team Will Make a Musical Out of "Far From Heaven"', *The New York Times*, 17 December. Online: http://artsbeat.blogs.nytimes.com/2010/12/17/grey-gardens-team-will-make-a-musical-out-of-far-from-heaven/ (accessed 24 December 2010).

Hebron, Sandra (2003), 'Haynes's Manual', *The Guardian*, 21 February. Online: www.guardian.co.uk/film/2003/feb/21/features (accessed 20 December 2010).

Higgins, Scott (2007), 'Orange and Blue, Desire and Loss: The Colour Score in *Far from Heaven*' in James Morrison (ed.), *The Cinema of Todd Haynes: All That Heaven Allows*, London: Wallflower, pp. 101–13.

Higson, Andrew (1991), 'Film Acting and Independent Cinema' in Jeremy G. Butler (ed.), *Star Texts: Image and Performance in Film and Television*, Detroit: Wayne State University Press, pp. 155–82.

Hilderbrand, Lucas (2002), review of *Far from Heaven*, *PopMatters*. Online: http://popmatters.com/film/reviews/f/far-from-heaven.shtml?_r=true (accessed 23 December 2010).

Hoberman, J. (2002), 'Signs of the Times', *The Village Voice*, 5 November. Online: www.villagevoice.com/2002-11-05/film/signs-of-the-times/1/ (accessed 26 August 2010).

Hoberman, J. and Jonathan Rosenbaum (1983), *Midnight Movies*, New York: Da Capo.

Holmlund, Christine (2005), 'Introduction: From the Margins to the Mainstream' in Christine Holmlund and Justin Wyatt (eds), *Contemporary American Independent Film: From the Margins to the Mainstream*, London: Routledge, pp. 1–19.

Horsley, Jake (2008), 'Obsessions into Light: Guy Maddin Interview', *Film and Festivals*. Online: www.filmandfestivals.com/index.php?option=com_content&view=article&id=3:obsessions-into-light (accessed 24 August 2010).

Hunter, Stephen (2002), 'He Likes Ike, and She Loves Raymond', *The Washington Post*, 15 November, p. C01. Online at www.washingtonpost.com/ac2/wp-dyn/A57205-2002Nov14 (accessed 20 August 2010).

Hutcheon, Linda (1989), *The Politics of Postmodernism*, London: Routledge.

James, Nick (2003), interview with Todd Haynes, *Sight and Sound*, Vol. 13, Issue 3 (March), pp. 14–15.

Jameson, Fredric (1991), *Postmodernism, Or the Cultural Logic of Late Capitalism*, Durham, NC: Duke University Press.

Johnson, Jeff (2005), *William Inge and the Subversion of Gender: Rewriting Stereotypes in the Plays, Novels, and Screenplays*, New York: McFarland.

Joyrich, Lynne (2004), 'Written on the Screen: Mediation and Immersion in *Far from Heaven*', *Camera Obscura*, 57, Vol. 19, No. 3, pp. 186–219.

Kaufman, Anthony (2002), 'Interview: Imitation of Film: Todd Haynes Mimics Melodrama in *Far from Heaven*', indieWIRE, 1 November. Online: www.indiewire.com/article/decade_todd_haynes_on_far_from_heaven/ (accessed 20 August 2010).

King, Geoff (2005), *American Independent Cinema*, London: I. B. Tauris.

King, Geoff (2009), *Indiewood, USA: Where Hollywood Meets Independent Cinema*, London: I. B. Tauris.

Kleinhans, Chuck (1998), 'Independent Features: Hopes and Dreams', in Jon Lewis (ed.), *The New American Cinema*, Durham, NC: Duke University Press, pp. 307–27.

Klinger, Barbara (1994), *Melodrama and Meaning: History, Culture, and the Films of Douglas Sirk*, Bloomington: Indiana University Press.

La Bruce, Bruce (1995), 'Pee Wee Herman: The Homosexual Subtext' in Corey K. Creekmur and Alexander Doty (eds), *Out in Culture: Gay, Lesbian, and Queer Essays on Popular Culture*, London: Cassell, pp. 382–8.

Lang, Robert (2002), *Masculine Interests: Homoerotics in Hollywood Film*, New York: Columbia University Press.

Levy, Emanuel (1999), *Cinema of Outsiders: The Rise of American Independent Film*, New York: New York University Press.

Love, Heather (2009), *Feeling Backward: Loss and the Politics of Queer Theory*, New York: Harvard University Press.

Luciano, Dana (2007), 'Coming Around Again: The Queer Momentum of *Far from Heaven*', *GLQ*, Vol. 13, Nos 2–3, pp. 249–72.

Lyons, Donald (1994), *Independent Visions: A Critical Introduction to Recent Independent American Film*, New York: Ballantine.

McCarthy, Todd (2007), review of *I'm Not There*, *Variety*, 4 September. Online: www.variety.com/review/VE1117934602.html?categoryid=31&cs=1&p=0 (accessed 27 August 2010).

Mayne, Judith (1993), *Cinema and Spectatorship*, London: Routledge.

Mendelsohn, Daniel (2003), 'The Melodramatic Moment', *The New York Times*, 23 March. Online at www.nytimes.com (accessed 20 August 2010).

Mercer, John and Martin Shingler (2004), *Melodrama: Genre, Style, Sensibility*, London: Wallflower.

Morrison, James (2007a), 'Todd Haynes in Theory and Practice' in Morrison (ed.), *The Cinema of Todd Haynes: All That Heaven Allows*, London: Wallflower, pp. 132–44.

Morrison, James (2007b), 'Introduction' in Morrison (ed.), *The Cinema of Todd Haynes: All That Heaven Allows*, London: Wallflower, pp. 1–6.

Moverman, Oren (1996), 'And All is Well in our World – Making *Safe*: Todd Haynes, Julianne Moore and Christine Vachon' in John Boorman and Walter Donohue (eds), *Projections 5: Film-makers on Film-making*, London: Faber & Faber, pp. 198–233.

Mulvey, Laura (1975), 'Visual Pleasure and Narrative Cinema', *Screen*, Vol. 16, Issue 3, pp. 6–18.

Mulvey, Laura (1987), 'Notes on Sirk and Melodrama' in Christine Gledhill (ed.), *Home is Where the Heart is: Studies in Melodrama and the Woman's Film*, London: BFI, pp. 75–9.

Mulvey, Laura (2003), review of *Far from Heaven*, *Sight and Sound*, Vol. 13, Issue 3 (March), pp. 40–1.

Neale, Steve (1986), 'Melodrama and Tears', *Screen*, Vol. 27, Issue 6, pp. 6–23.

Neale, Steve (1993), 'Melo Talk: On the Meaning and Use of the Term "Melodrama" in the American Trade Press', *Velvet Light Trap*, Fall, pp. 66–89.

Needham, Gary (2010), *Brokeback Mountain*, Edinburgh: Edinburgh University Press.

Negra, Diane (2005), ' "Queen of the Indies": Parker Posey's Niche Stardom and the Taste Cultures of Independent Film' in Christine Holmlund and Justin Wyatt (eds), *Contemporary American Independent Film: From the Margins to the Mainstream*, London: Routledge, pp. 71–88.

Nowell-Smith, Geoffrey (1987), 'Minnelli and Melodrama' in Christine Gledhill (ed.), *Home is Where the Heart is: Studies in Melodrama and the Woman's Film*, London: BFI, pp. 70–4.

Nunokawa, Jeff (1991), '"All the Sad Young Men": AIDS and the Work of Mourning' in Diana Fuss (ed.), *Inside/Out: Lesbian Theories, Gay Theories*, London: Routledge, pp. 311–23.

O'Brien, Geoffrey (2002), 'Past Perfect', *Artforum*, November, pp. 152–6, 202.

O'Hehir, Andrew (2002), review of *Far from Heaven*, *Salon*, 8 November. Online: www.salon.com/entertainment/movies/review/2002/11/08/far_from_heaven (accessed 20 August 2010).

Oliver, Mary Beth (1993), 'Exploring the Paradox of the Enjoyment of Sad Films', *Human Communication Research*, Vol. 19, No. 3 (March), pp. 315–42.

Pierson, John (1997), *Spike, Mike, Slackers & Dykes: A Guided Tour Across a Decade of Independent American Cinema*, London: Faber & Faber.

Plantinga, Carl (1999), 'The Scene of Empathy and the Human Face on Film' in Carl Plantinga and Greg M. Smith (eds), *Passionate Views: Film, Cognition, and Emotion*, Baltimore: Johns Hopkins University Press, pp. 239–56.

Rhodes, John David (2007), 'Allegory, *Mise-en-scène*, AIDS: Interpreting *Safe*' in James Morrison (ed.), *The Cinema of Todd Haynes: All That Heaven Allows*, London: Wallflower, pp. 68–78.

Rich, B. Ruby (1992), 'New Queer Cinema', *Sight and Sound*, Vol. 2, No. 5 (September), pp. 32–5.

Rich, B. Ruby (2005), 'Tell it to the Camera', *Sight and Sound*, Vol. 15, Issue 4 (April), pp. 32–5.

Roof, Judith (2002), *All About Thelma and Eve: Sidekicks and Third Wheels*, Urbana: University of Illinois Press.

Rosen, David with Peter Hamilton (1990), *Off-Hollywood: The Making and Marketing of Independent Films*, New York: Grove Weidenfeld.

Rosenbaum, Jonathan (1998), 'Hack Job', *Chicago Reader*. Online: www.chireader.com/movies/archives/1998/1298/12258.html (accessed 20 August 2010).

Rosenbaum, Jonathan (2002), 'Magnificent Repression', *Chicago Reader*, 21 November. Online: www.chicagoreader.com/chicago/magnificent-repression/Content?oid=910451 (accessed 20 August 2010).

Rosenbaum, Jonathan (2004), *Essential Cinema: On the Necessity of Film Canons*, Baltimore: Johns Hopkins University Press.

Russo, Vito (1981), *The Celluloid Closet: Homosexuality in the Movies*, New York: Harper & Row.

Sallitt, Dan, undated review of *Far from Heaven*. Online: www.24fpsmagazine.com (accessed 20 August 2010).

Sedgwick, Eve (1993), *Tendencies*, London: Duke University Press.

Shattuc, Jane (1995), *Television, Tabloids and Tears: Fassbinder and Popular Culture*, Minneapolis: University of Minnesota Press.

Simon, Alex (2008), 'Patricia Clarkson: Belle of the Ball'. Online at http://the hollywoodinterview.blogspot.com (accessed 16 August 2010).

Singer, Ben (1990), 'Female Power in the Serial Queen Melodrama: The Etiology of an Anomaly', *Camera Obscura*, 22, Vol. 8, No. 1, pp. 90–129.

Smith, Jack (1962–3), 'The Perfect Filmic Appositeness of Maria Montez', *Film Culture*, Issue 27, pp. 28–32.

Smith, Jeff (1999), 'Movie Music as Moving Music: Emotion, Cognition, and the Film Score' in Carl Plantinga and Greg M. Smith (eds), *Passionate Views: Film, Cognition, and Emotion*, Baltimore: Johns Hopkins University Press, pp. 146–67.

Sontag, Susan (1966), 'Notes on "Camp"' in Sontag, *Against Interpretation*, New York: Farrar, Straus & Giroux, pp. 275–92.

Spargo, Tamsin (1999), *Foucault and Queer Theory*, Cambridge: Icon.

Stacey, Jackie (1992), 'Desperately Seeking Difference' in Mandy Merck/Screen (ed.), *The Sexual Subject: A Screen Reader in Sexuality*, London: Routledge, pp. 244–57.

Staiger, Janet (2004), 'Authorship Studies and Gus Van Sant', *Film Criticism*, Vol. 29, No. 1, pp. 1–22.

Sterritt, David (2002), '*Heaven* Almost Perfect', *Christian Science Monitor*, 8 November. Online: www.csmonitor.com/2002/1108/p15s02-almo.html (accessed 26 August 2010).

Sullivan, Robert (2007), 'This is not a Bob Dylan Movie', *New York Times*, 7 October. Online: www.nytimes.com/2007/10/07/magazine/07Haynes. html?_r=1 (accessed 20 August 2010).

Taubin, Amy (1996), 'Nowhere to Hide', *Sight and Sound*, Vol. 6, No. 5 (May), pp. 32–4.

Taubin, Amy (2002), 'In Every Dream Home', *Film Comment*, Vol. 38, No. 5 (September/October), pp. 22–4, 26.

Taylor, Ella (2002) 'Get Out Your Handkerchiefs: Todd Haynes' Postmodern Tearjerker', *L.A. Weekly*. Online: http://toddhaynes.wolfzen.com/text/ ffh_int07.shtml (accessed 25 March 2010).

Terry, Jennifer (1991), 'Theorising Deviant Historiography', *differences*, Vol. 3, No. 2, pp. 55–74.

Tobias, Scott (2008), interview with Julianne Moore, *The AV Club*, 28 May. Online: www.avclub.com/articles/julianne-moore,14247/ (accessed 20 August 2010).

Tyler, Parker (1972), *Screening the Sexes: Homosexuality in the Movies*, New York: Holt, Rinehart & Winston.

Tzioumakis, Yannis (2006), *American Independent Cinema: An Introduction*, Edinburgh: Edinburgh University Press.

Uhlich, Keith (2002), 'Todd Haynes', *Senses of Cinema*. Online: http://archive. sensesofcinema.com/contents/directors/02/haynes.html   (accessed   25 August 2010).

Vachon, Christine (1998), *Shooting to Kill: How an Independent Producer Blasts Through the Barriers to Make Movies that Matter*, London: Bloomsbury.

Vachon, Christine (2006), *A Killer Life: How an Independent Film Producer Survives Deals and Disasters in Hollywood and Beyond*, New York: Simon & Schuster.

Warhol, Robyn (2003), *Having A Good Cry: Effeminate Feelings and Pop-Culture Forms*, Columbus: Ohio State University Press.

Waters, John (1991), *Shock Value: A Tasteful Book About Bad Taste*, London: Fourth Estate.

Weiss, Andrea (1992), *Vampires and Violets: Lesbians in the Cinema*, London: Jonathan Cape/Random House.

Whatling, Clare (1997), *Screen Dreams: Fantasising Lesbians in Film*, Manchester: Manchester University Press.

White, Patricia (1995), 'Supporting Character: The Queer Career of Agnes Moorehead' in Corey K. Creekmur and Alexander Doty (eds), *Out in Culture: Gay, Lesbian, and Queer Essays on Popular Culture*, London: Cassell, pp. 91–114.

White, Patricia (1999), *Uninvited: Classical Hollywood Cinema and Lesbian Representability*, Bloomington: Indiana University Press.

Willemen, Paul (1971), 'Distanciation and Douglas Sirk', *Screen*, Vol. 12, Issue 2 (Summer), pp. 63–7.

Willis, Sharon (2003), 'The Politics of Disappointment: Todd Haynes Rewrites Douglas Sirk', *Camera Obscura*, 54, Vol. 18, Number 3, pp. 130–75.

Wood, Robin (1978), 'Responsibilities of a Gay Film Critic', *Film Comment*, Vol. 14, No. 1 (January/February), pp. 12–17.

Wyatt, Justin (1998a), *Poison*, Trowbridge: Flicks.

Wyatt, Justin (1998b), 'The Formation of the 'Major Independent': Miramax, New Line and the New Hollywood', in Steve Neale and Murray Smith (eds), *Contemporary Hollywood Cinema*, London: Routledge, pp. 74–90.

Index

Page numbers in italics refer to images

Tarantino, Quentin, 7, 10, 11, 35,
    41, 55
Tarnation, 16
Tea and Sympathy, 94, 95
Three Faces of Eve, The, 55, 60
Turner, Lana, 57, 95, 98
2012, 15, 54

USA Films, 12, 17, 18, 19, 20, 24, 36

Vachon, Christine, 4, 5, 16, 17, 18,
    23, 42, 82, 131
Van Sant, Gus, 5, 15, 22, 48, 50, 52,
    53, 54

Velvet Goldmine, 2, 4, 5, 16, 17, 24,
    43, 44, 48, 49, 63, 65, 130, 131,
    133n5

Waking Life, 31, *32*
Walk to Remember, A, 75, 76, 77
Warhol, Andy, 28, 108, 111
Waters, John, 16, 26, 27, 109, 111
Weinstein, Harvey, 17, 131
Weston, Celia, 25, 101, 112, 117
Williams, Tennessee, 94, 95, 111
Written on the Wind, 2, 35, 57, 67, 68,
    72, 75, 77, 96, 122
Wyman, Jane, 37, 56, 93, 98, 124